# CONTENTS

M000112021

SAMPLE LESSON

# To the Student

Strange things that cannot be explained happen to people every day. Haunted houses, unexplainable phobias, and deaths occurring under suspicious circumstances have confounded people for hundreds of years. The stories in *On the Edge: Scared Stiff* go deep into the mysteries of true crime, unsolved mysteries, and adventure. Anthrax is sent anonymously through the mail. A woman is kidnapped during a war in the Middle East. Sailors are rescued in the midst of a ferocious storm on the high seas. Stalkers terrorize celebrities. Many of these crimes remain unsolved. You might be the person to crack the case.

As you read the stories in this book, you will be developing your reading skills. The lessons will help you increase your reading speed while you improve your reading comprehension, critical thinking skills, and vocabulary. Many of the exercises are similar to questions you will see on state and national tests. Learning how to complete them will help you prepare for tests you will take in the future. Some of the exercises encourage you to write sentence or paragraph responses. As you write your opinions, you will learn to support them with specific examples from the stories you read.

You may not believe that ghosts actually haunt houses. You may think agoraphobia is too strange to actually happen in real life. You might see a clue the police have missed in the unsolved case of the Tylenol murders. One thing is for certain: you won't be able to take your eyes off each page until you've read the book cover to cover.

# How to Use This Book

**ABOUT THE BOOK** *On the Edge: Scared Stiff* has ten units, each of which contains two stories and a lesson. The stories are about true crime, unsolved mysteries, and ordinary people who do very bizarre things. Each story is followed by a page of reading comprehension exercises. These exercises will help you to better understand the article. At the end of each unit are exercises that help develop vocabulary and critical thinking skills. These exercises will assist your understanding of the similarities between the two stories and will help you relate them to your own experiences.

**THE SAMPLE LESSON** The first lesson in the book is a sample that demonstrates how the units are organized. The sample lesson will show you how to complete the exercises. The correct answers to the questions are included.

**WORKING THROUGH EACH UNIT** Begin each unit by looking at the photograph. Before you begin reading, think about your reaction to the photo and predict what you think the article might be about. Then read the article.

Sometimes you or your teacher may want to time how long it takes you to read a story. You can write your time in the circle at the end of each story. Use the Words-per-Minute Table on page 120 to find your reading speed and record it on the Plotting Your Progress graph on page 121. As you read through the book, you will be able to watch your reading speed improve on the graph.

After you read the article and record your speed, begin the exercises. The comprehension section will test your understanding of what you have read. The vocabulary exercises will include words that were used in both stories. The critical thinking exercises will help you build analytical skills. Some of the exercises will ask you to write a paragraph giving your thoughts and opinions about the stories. Answers to all of the exercises can be found in the *On the Edge Teacher's Guide.*

SAMPLE LESSON

SELECTION 1

## Sneaky Snakes

# ON THE EDGE
## SCARED STIFF

**Henry Billings**
**Melissa Billings**

Series Editor: Amy Collins
Executive Editor: Linda Kwil
Production Manager: Genevieve Kelley
Marketing Manager: Sean Klunder
Cover Design: Michael E. Kelly

**McGraw-Hill
Contemporary**

Copyright © 2003 by McGraw-Hill/Contemporary, a business unit of The McGraw-Hill
Companies, Inc. No part of this book may be reproduced, stored in a retrieval system,
or transmitted by any means, electronic, mechanical, photocopying, recording,
or otherwise, without prior permission of the publisher.

Send all inquiries to:
McGraw-Hill/Contemporary
130 East Randolph Street, Suite 400
Chicago, Illinois 60601

ISBN: 0-07-285198-8

Printed in the United States of America.

1 2 3 4 5 6 7 8 9 10  QPD  08 07 06 05 04 03

The **McGraw·Hill** Companies

To keep track of your reading speed, write down your starting time before you begin the selection. At the end of the selection, record how long it took you to read the story. You can find out how many words per minute you are reading by using the table on page 120. Watch your speed improve by using the chart on page 121.

Hope Loyd was not looking for trouble. All she wanted to do was walk her dog. It was late in the evening on May 18, 1997. She had just stepped outside her apartment in Dallas, Texas. Suddenly she felt something nip her left ankle. She thought it was just a thorn. But when she reached down to pull it out, she saw what it really was. A poisonous copperhead snake was curled up beside her.

Her foot began to turn numb. Loyd raced up the stairs to her home. "I was pretty calm until I got into the apartment," she said later, "and then I started screaming: 'A snake bit me! A snake bit me!'"

Her husband and sister rushed her to the hospital. The doctors treated her and sent her home. Loyd was lucky. A copperhead's venom is not very strong. Also, the snake bit her right on the bone. If the snake had bitten into a vein or artery, the bite could have been fatal. The incident left Loyd nervous about a second attack. "I'm frightened to walk my dog again," she said. "It scared me to see a snake coiled beside me."

Snake attacks often come when they are least expected. In 2002, a woman was bitten when she turned on an outdoor water faucet. She didn't see the snake lying in the grass. In Colorado, a rattlesnake bit an eleven-year-old boy who was out riding his bike. The boy put his foot down to stop on the street in front of his house. He didn't notice the snake lying on the ground.

Like Hope Loyd, most people want nothing to do with poisonous snakes. But Teddy Tarrant was different. This South Carolina man kept one for a pet. He didn't keep just any old snake. Tarrant kept a Pakistani black snake. A member of the cobra family, the Pakistani black snake is one of the deadliest snakes in the world. It produces enough venom to kill ten people.

For two years, Tarrant had no problems. Then, on July 4, 2001, he paid the price for keeping such a snake as a pet. Tarrant and his brother-in-law were taking pictures. They wanted one with Tarrant rubbing the back of the snake's neck. But when Tarrant reached out his hand, the snake sensed a threat. It struck with lightning speed. "I saw it," Tarrant said. "It felt like being stung by a little bee. It startled me. It scared me."

Tarrant was taken to a hospital in Greenville, South Carolina. But there wasn't much that the doctors could do for him. Cobra bites are rare in the United States. Most hospitals don't keep the antidote for such bites on hand. Without the right anti-venom medicine, Tarrant would die.

The nearest hospital that could treat Tarrant was in Miami. By the time he was rushed there, he could not move his arms or legs. He was not breathing on his own. Luckily, the anti-venom medicine worked. Soon Tarrant was able to move his limbs and breathe freely once more.

Would he do it again? "I want to keep the snake," said Tarrant, "but I don't think my wife is going to let me."

Keeping a snake like that as a pet was a bad idea. "I'm not even going to use the term 'pet' because it and 'cobra' don't fit in the same sentence," said Nigel Platt, a snake expert. "You are dealing with a life-threatening, dangerous, wild animal."

A person who gets bitten by a snake once is unlucky. One who gets bitten twice is really unlucky. But what do you call someone who gets bitten *three* times in less than *four* months? That's what happened to Jay Vaughn. He worked at the Saratoga Jungle Gardens in Florida. It was his job to handle snakes. But in January of 2001, a copperhead bite sent him to the hospital. He was the first snakebite victim at Jungle Gardens in twenty-two years.

In March, a diamondback rattlesnake bit Vaughn. Again, he was rushed to the hospital. This time, Jungle Gardens fired him. No competent snake handler gets bitten twice in three months.

But the story wasn't over. Vaughn kept a gaboon viper at home. Its venom is so powerful it can kill an elephant. Vaughn called his pet snake "Fangs." That was an apt name, because the gaboon viper has longer fangs than any other snake in the world.

On April 3, Vaughn was trying to feed Fangs when the snake bit him on the right hand. He was lucky to survive. Anti-venom medicine does not work well when used too often. A person's body builds up a tolerance for it. So Vaughn was in greater danger than a first-time victim would have been.

Florida officials had had enough. They decided that Vaughn and snakes didn't mix. They took away the snake that bit him. They also took away a second viper he was keeping at home. As the case of Jay Vaughn shows, being afraid of snakes is sometimes better than being fearless.

When you finish reading, subtract your start time from your end time. This is how long it took you to read the selection. Enter your reading time below.

If you have been timed while reading this article, enter your reading time below. Then turn to the Words-per-Minute Table on page 120 and look up your reading speed (words per minute). Enter your reading speed on the graph on page 121.

**Reading Time:** Selection 1

_____ : _____
MINUTES    SECONDS

Work through the exercises on this page.
If necessary, refer back to the story.

## UNDERSTANDING IDEAS Circle the letter of the best answer.

**1. As a result of Hope Loyd's experience with a copperhead snake, she**

A decided to get a pet snake

B got over her fear of snakes

C *was afraid of taking her dog out for a walk*

D moved out of her home

**2. Snakes have a reputation for being sneaky because**

F they produce deadly venom

G they are rarely seen in the United States

H they enjoy being someone's pet

J *they strike without warning*

**3. Proof that Teddy Tarrant hadn't really learned a lesson is that**

A *he wanted to keep his pet snake*

B he nearly died

C he recovered from his snake bite

D he did not listen to his wife

**4. Jay Vaughn lost his job at Jungle Gardens because**

F he was afraid of snakes

G he had his own pet snake at home

H *he was not a good snake handler*

J he was not allowed to handle snakes

**5. Based on the information in the article, the reader can conclude that anti-venom medicine**

A is dangerous for most people

B *is the only cure for a deadly snake bite*

C doesn't work on most people

D is available in most hospitals

## SUMMARIZE For each blank, choose the word that best completes the meaning of the paragraph.

| poisonous | afraid | strike |
|-----------|--------|--------|
| medicine  | keep   | experts |

Most people are _____*afraid*_____ of

snakes—and for good reason. Snakes often

_____*strike*_____ without warning.

But some people like snakes so much that they

_____*keep*_____ them as pets. A bite from a

_____*poisonous*_____ snake can kill a person.

Teddy Tarrant and Jay Vaughn would have died if they

hadn't been given anti-venom _____*medicine*_____.

It's best to leave snakes in the hands of

_____*experts*_____.

## IF YOU WERE THERE Imagine that a member of your family wanted to keep a pet snake. Write a brief paragraph explaining what you would tell him or her. Be sure to include examples from the story to support your response.

*I would tell the person that it is extremely dangerous to*

*keep a snake as a pet. Eventually, someone will be bitten.*

*Teddy Tarrant had a pet snake. He almost died when he*

*was bitten. Jay Vaughn had no fear of his pet snake either,*

*until the snake bit him and he nearly lost his life!*

**Read the next article and complete the exercises that follow.**

3

# Rats Everywhere

They can't see well, but they have great hearing and a keen sense of smell. They have short hair, scaly tails, and big appetites. Their teeth are so strong they can chew through wood, bones, and even concrete. They are rats, and in cities around the world they are a fact of life.

"Wherever humans are, [there'll] be rats," says pest control expert Will Wagner. "They don't go where there's no food." Indeed, most rats like to stay within 150 feet of their nests. So that means getting up close and personal with their human neighbors.

Some people joke about the presence of rats in cities. New York talk show host David Letterman once joked, "It was so hot today, the rats at Dunkin' Donuts moved over to Ben and Jerry's." Another time he joked, "It was so sunny, rats were coming up out of the subway squinting."

But for many people, rats are no joking matter. For one thing, rats bite. Just ask Manuel Muñoz. He lived next to a restaurant on 171st Street in New York City. The scraps of food left on the ground brought in an army of rats. One night, a rat entered Muñoz's bedroom and bit him on the wrist while he slept. It left quite a scar. Muñoz feared that rats would crawl into his infant son's crib. So he waited up at night with a metal bar in his hand, ready to fend the creatures off.

Rose Madera lived in the same building as Muñoz. The rats terrified her and her two-year-old daughter. "At night, [I] hear them screaming between the walls," Madera said. "The rats often wake my daughter by pulling at her door."

It's not just poor neighborhoods that are plagued by rats. The rodents are everywhere. In New York rats are in the subways. They're in empty lots, slums, and old warehouses. But they are also in Central Park. They're in churches and stores. They're in fancy Upper East Side homes.

No one knows how many rats live in New York City. For many years, experts claimed that there was one rat for every person. That meant that the city had about eight million rats. In 2001, some experts said the number was really closer to twenty-five million. That meant there were three rats for every person.

Other cities have rat problems, too. One man described the rats around his Detroit home. "It's pretty bad," he said. "Every night, you can see them running across the lawn. They come from house to house to house." In Washington, D.C., Noam Brown noted, "When night falls, they own the alley. You open the door and step out and . . . the rats will turn and glare at you."

People fear the pain of a rat bite. But a bigger danger comes from the diseases the rats spread. They carry as many as thirty-five diseases. Many of these diseases are lethal. Experts say that over the last thousand years, diseases carried by rats have killed more people than all the world's wars.

So far, few Americans have died from rat-borne diseases. Still, people view rats with fear and loathing. That is especially true when the rats show up in unexpected places. In 1999, Meryle Secrest moved to a nice part of Washington, D.C. One day she saw an animal "about the size of a small cat" near her bird feeder. Secrest got out her binoculars. She took a closer look. "Only then did I realize I was looking at a rat," she said. "I was absolutely horrified. I had not realized I was moving into an area where rats visit bird feeders in broad daylight."

Rats also roam the sewer system. If they stayed there, it wouldn't be too bad. But one Washington, D.C., couple reported that a rat floated up into their toilet bowl!

New Yorker Elisa Reyes found a rat looking at her from inside her laundry basket. She said, "Now I'm scared to go down [to the laundry room] and use the washing machine."

Rats also spooked Susan Pietrzyk. One day she was walking down the back stairs of her home. All at once a horde of rats appeared. They raced right over her feet. Pietrzyk was so unnerved that she stopped using that staircase.

Some cities have formed Rat Patrols. These groups have one job—to kill as many rats as they can. In 2001, New York launched an all-out war on the city's rats. The mayor named a "Rat Czar" to head the effort. Meetings were held at Columbia University to discuss the rat problem. The city even came up with an advertising campaign. People were urged not to leave scraps of food where rats could eat them. The slogan was "You Feed Them, You Breed Them."

A year later, New York pest control agent Larry Adams was asked who was winning the war. "Nobody's winning," said Adams. "But we're not losing." When it comes to fighting rats, "not losing" may be as good as it gets.

If you have been timed while reading this article, enter your reading time below. Then turn to the Words-per-Minute Table on page 120 and look up your reading speed (words per minute). Enter your reading speed on the graph on page 121.

**Reading Time:** Selection 2

_____ : _____
MINUTES      SECONDS

**UNDERSTANDING IDEAS** Circle the letter of the best answer.

**1. Which statement about rats is NOT true?**
A Rats have very strong teeth.
B Rats spread diseases.
C Rats have a good sense of smell.
D Most people are glad to have rats in their city.

**2. Rats are found in most cities because**
F it is harder to catch a rat in a city than in the country
G cities have many good sources of food
H city people do not mind the presence of rats
J rats enjoy being around a lot of people

**3. Some cities have formed Rat Patrols to**
A educate children
B kill as many rats as they can find
C keep rats in the sewer systems
D encourage people to breed rats

**4. Based on the information in the article, which statement is true?**
F Comedians often joke about real problems.
G Rats carry diseases that can kill people.
H In New York City, there are more rats than people.
J All of the above

**SUMMARIZE** For each blank, choose the word that best completes the meaning of the paragraph.

| food | cities | diseases |
| rats | bite | rich |

Wherever there are people, there will be

_____. Rats have big appetites and

they can chew through wood, bones, and concrete in

search of _____. Rats are

everywhere in big _____. They can

be found in subways, empty lots, and in both poor and

_____ neighborhoods. Rats

_____ people, but the biggest danger

comes from the _____ they spread.

**IF YOU WERE THERE** Write a brief paragraph explaining some of the things you could do to keep rats away from your home. Be sure to include examples from the story to support your response.

_____
_____
_____
_____
_____
_____

7

**USE CONTEXT CLUES** When you read, you may find a word whose meaning is unfamiliar to you. When that happens, you can look up the word's meaning in the dictionary. You can also find out what the word means by looking for context clues. These are words or sentences that come before or after the word. Context clues can be antonyms or synonyms of the unfamiliar word. They may also be an example or definition of the unfamiliar word.

Read each excerpt from the stories you just read. Circle the letter with the best meaning of the underlined word.

1. **Most hospitals don't keep the <u>antidote</u> for such bites on hand. Without the right anti-venom medicine, Tarrant would die.**
   A  special bandages and equipment
   B  expert snake handler
   C  material used to wrap and protect the hand
   D  medicine that reverses the effect of poison

2. **Vaughn called his pet snake "Fangs." That was an <u>apt</u> name because the gaboon viper has the longest fangs of any snake in the world.**
   F  bad
   G  inappropriate
   H  fitting
   J  silly

3. **So far, few Americans have died from rat-borne diseases. Still, people view rats with fear and <u>loathing</u>. . . . "I was absolutely horrified."**
   A  total respect
   B  awe
   C  extreme dislike
   D  guilt

4. **Again, he was rushed to the hospital. This time Jungle Gardens fired him. No <u>competent</u> snake handler gets bitten twice in three months.**
   F  capable
   G  forgetful
   H  fearless
   J  unqualified

5. **They carry as many as 35 diseases. Many are <u>lethal</u>. Experts say that over the last thousand years, diseases carried by rats have killed more people than all the world's wars.**
   A  unimportant
   B  deadly
   C  mildly harmful
   D  not life-threatening

**PUT WORDS INTO CONTEXT** Complete the paragraph using the underlined words from the exercise on this page.

The sight of a snake or rat fills most people with

_____. That is a wise and

_____ response. A bite from a

poisonous snake can be _____.

A person would die unless given the right

_____ in time. Stay away from rats

and snakes. Leave them to _____

experts who are trained to deal with them.

**SYNONYMS** A synonym is a word that has the same, or nearly the same, meaning as another word. For example, *smart* and *clever* are synonyms.

Circle the letter of the word or phrase that has almost the SAME meaning as the underlined word.

1. **It produces enough <u>venom</u> to kill ten humans.**

   **A** bite

   **B** disease

   **C** poison

   **D** power

2. **When Tarrant reached out his hand, the snake sensed a <u>threat</u>.**

   **F** human

   **G** possible danger

   **H** poison

   **J** bite

3. **Rats also <u>roam</u> the sewer system.**

   **A** avoid, stay away from

   **B** float

   **C** walk around in

   **D** leave

4. **Susan Pietrzyk was so <u>unnerved</u> that she stopped using that set of stairs.**

   **F** calm

   **G** courageous

   **H** upset

   **J** tired

5. **All at once, a <u>horde</u> of rats appeared.**

   **A** small amount of

   **B** family

   **C** neighborhood

   **D** a large group

**SYNONYM ANALOGIES** Analogies show relationships between words. Synonym analogies show patterns between words that have similar meanings. For example, *big* is to *large* as *little* is to *small*. For each blank, choose an underlined word from the exercise on this page to correctly complete the analogy.

1. *Courageous* is to *brave* as

   _____ is to *disturbed*.

2. *Group* is to *bunch* as

   _____ is to *crowd*.

3. *Listen* is to *hear* as

   _____ is to *wander*.

4. *Medicine* is to *antidote* as

   _____ is to *poison*.

5. *Same* is to *equal* as

   _____ is to *danger*.

**ORGANIZE IDEAS** The main ideas in a story are the larger, more general topics that are covered. The specific details are the facts that clarify or support the main ideas. Fill in the chart by using the items listed at the right. If the bulleted item is a main idea from the story, write it in the row marked "Main Idea." If the item is a detail that supports the main idea, write it in the row marked "Detail."

| "Sneaky Snakes" |
| --- |
| **Main Idea:** |
| Detail: |
| Detail: |
| Detail: |
| Detail: |

| "Rats Everywhere" |
| --- |
| **Main Idea:** |
| Detail: |
| Detail: |
| Detail: |
| Detail: |

- Poisonous snakes should not be kept as pets.

- Hope Loyd was bitten by a snake when she left her apartment.

- David Letterman often jokes about New York City's rats.

- Some cities have formed Rat Patrols.

- Anti-venom medicines shouldn't be used too often.

- Teddy Tarrant couldn't move his arms or legs after he was bitten by his pet snake.

- Experts think there are three rats for every one person in New York.

- Rats carry lethal diseases.

- Jay Vaughn was bitten by a snake three times.

- Rats live and breed wherever there are people.

**SUPPORT THE MAIN IDEA** Write a paragraph about dangerous animals. State the main idea in the first sentence. Then use details from both stories to support your main idea.

_____

_____

_____

_____

_____

_____

**DRAW CONCLUSIONS** A conclusion is a judgment based on information. The way you draw a conclusion is to think about what you've read and see if you can make a judgment, or general statement, about it. Read the paragraph below about Jay Vaughn. Then choose the best answer to each question.

[1] Jay Vaughn got a job handling snakes at Saratoga Jungle Gardens in Florida. [2] He lost his job because he got bitten twice in just three months. [3] Then he was bitten a third time by one of his own pet snakes. [4] Vaughn was lucky to survive because anti-venom medicine does not work well when used too often. [5] Florida officials decided to take away both of Vaughn's pet snakes.

1. **Which conclusion can you draw based on the paragraph above?**
   **A** The officials had no right to take away Vaughn's pet.
   **B** The officials were more concerned about Vaughn's well-being than he was.
   **C** Jay Vaughn was good at his job.
   **D** It doesn't matter how many snake bites a person gets; he can always be cured.

2. **Which sentence from the paragraph explains why frequent snake bites can be dangerous?**
   **F** Sentence 1
   **G** Sentence 2
   **H** Sentence 3
   **J** Sentence 4

3. **What other conclusion can you draw from the paragraph?**
   **A** Jay Vaughn was afraid of snakes.
   **B** Jay Vaughn should not get another job working with snakes.
   **C** Jay Vaughn was a careful man.
   **D** Jay Vaughn began thinking about what kind of snake to buy next.

**JUDGE THE EVIDENCE** When you make a conclusion, you must judge if the information presented is accurate or convincing. Choose the best answer.

1. **Which statement best supports the conclusion that rats are no joking matter?**
   **A** Rats have been around for thousands of years.
   **B** Rats carry deadly diseases.
   **C** Rats live wherever there are people.
   **D** Meetings were held at Columbia University to discuss New York's rat problem.

2. **Which statement best supports the conclusion that New York City takes its rat threat seriously?**
   **F** People fear the pain of a rat bite.
   **G** New York City has a "Rat Czar" in charge of getting rid of rats.
   **H** Rats are in all parts of the city.
   **J** David Letterman jokes about rats in the city.

**YOUR OWN CONCLUSION** Do snakes or rats pose the greater danger to people? State your conclusion and support it with examples from both stories.

_____

_____

_____

_____

SELECTION 1

# Mad with Fear

"I heard a door banging downstairs," said Michael Flatley. "The next moment, I heard a click. It was someone opening the bedroom door."

This happened at about 3:00 A.M. in early May of 2001. Flatley was sleeping in his mansion in southern France when he awoke and heard the noise. A world-famous dancer, Flatley had long worried that someone might invade his private life.

This often happens to celebrities. Overzealous fans follow stars wherever they go. The worst of these fans become stalkers. They are not content just to watch their favorite star dance or act or sing. They become so obsessed that they want to share the personal lives of their idols. If they are denied this, some stalkers turn violent. So Flatley—like many famous stars—hired bodyguards to protect him.

Yet on this night, a stalker somehow slipped into his home unseen. "My heart was hammering like a rabbit's," recalled Flatley. "I told myself I was imagining it, that I was being ridiculous."

He wasn't imagining anything. There was a full moon that night. Flatley could see the hallway that led to the bedroom. "Suddenly, a man's head came round the door," he said. "He stared straight at me. The hairs shot up on the back of my neck."

Flatley screamed at the intruder to get out of the house. But the man just stepped into the bedroom and stood at the foot of the bed. "I jumped out of bed and pulled on some trousers and shoes." By then, the stalker had moved back into the hallway. "He was standing there waiting for me," said Flatley. "I thought there was going to be a fight."

Flatley kept screaming at the man. At last, the stalker turned and fled. Flatley ran after him. But the man was too quick. He disappeared from view. Flatley ran into the hallway and began searching the whole house. He couldn't find the man anywhere. The police soon came. They could not find the intruder, either. Everyone agreed that the man wasn't a robber. Cash and credit cards, which were clearly visible, had not been touched.

The incident left Flatley badly shaken. "Nothing can describe the fear of waking up and seeing a complete stranger standing staring at you just six feet away," the dancer said. "The image and fear of that moment has stuck with me and left me frightened, mad, and vulnerable. It's the price I've paid for my fame, but what happened was terrifying—disgusting."

Flatley was also angry that the stalker had gotten past his guards. "I am still absolutely furious that this could happen," he said. "I spend a lot of money on security and it's a mystery how he managed to break-in."

Flatley decided he needed more protection. So he hired former FBI agents. They began guarding him twenty-four hours a day. He had laser beams installed all around his house. Flatley also took other measures which he refused to reveal. He knew that the stalker might be reading about him. Flatley wanted the man to know he had beefed up his security, but he didn't want to give away all the details.

"I've always had a high level of security to protect the many expensive things in my home," said Flatley. "Now I've invested heavily in security because fearing for my life is the biggest terror I believe I'll ever [face]."

Flatley tried to keep a low profile in his personal life. "I've spent more money trying to stay out of the papers than most stars spend trying to get into them," he said. "I haven't . . . encouraged obsessive fans. They've just turned up."

Indeed, soon after the intruder broke into his home, Flatley had to deal with another stalker. This time it was a German woman. For years she had tracked Flatley. She had followed him around the world. She had gone to many of his shows. When she found out where he lived, she sent him letters and flowers. In the summer of 2001, she started hanging around outside his London home. Flatley called the police. They warned the woman to stay away.

That seemed to work. But Flatley couldn't be sure. "I don't know what's going to happen from one minute to the next," he said. "I fear for my life at times, which is a very sad thing to happen." He added, "It's a disgrace that people can do this kind of thing. But I have to deal with it as best I can."

If you have been timed while reading this article, enter your reading time below. Then turn to the Words-per-Minute Table on page 120 and look up your reading speed (words per minute). Enter your reading speed on the graph on page 121.

**Reading Time:** Selection 1

_____ : _____
MINUTES        SECONDS

## UNDERSTANDING IDEAS Circle the letter of the best answer.

**1. Which statement belongs in the empty box?**

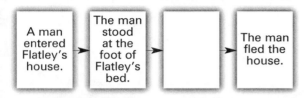

A Flatley and the man got into a fight.

B Flatley recognized his bodyguard.

C Flatley called the police.

D Flatley screamed at the man.

**2. Flatley always worried that**

F he would not have fans

G he would spend too much money on security

H someone might invade his privacy

J he would be a celebrity

**3. Because an intruder had gotten into Flatley's house, Flatley**

A moved away

B fired his guards

C added more security

D never recovered his valuables

**4. The German woman finally stopped hanging around Flatley's London home when**

F Flatley started to ignore her

G the police warned her to stay away

H Flatley invited her in

J newspapers wrote about her

## SUMMARIZE For each blank, choose the word that best completes the meaning of the paragraph.

| price | fears | intruder |
|-------|-------|----------|
| privacy | deal | London |

At times, Michael Flatley _____ for his life. It is the _____ he pays for fame. Stalkers have invaded the _____ of his home twice since May 2001. Flatley woke at 3:00 A.M. to find an _____ in his bedroom. On another occasion, an intruder stayed outside Flatley's _____ home until he called the police. Flatley doesn't encourage obsessive fans, but he's learning how to _____ with them.

## IF YOU WERE THERE What do you think you would do if someone were stalking you? Write a brief paragraph explaining your actions. Be sure to include examples from the story to support your response.

_____

_____

_____

_____

_____

# Tennis Love

Any fan of tennis during the 1990s will remember the attack. It happened on April 30, 1993. Monica Seles had sat down during a match in Germany. She was taking a short break while changing sides of the court. Seles took a drink and wiped her face with a towel. She didn't see Guenter Parche sneaking up behind her. To the horror of everyone, this "fan" plunged a knife into her back.

"I didn't want to kill her," declared Parche at his trial. "I just wanted to hurt her slightly so that Monica wouldn't be able to play for a couple of weeks." It turned out that Parche was in love with one of Monica's rivals, Steffi Graf. He filled his room with pictures of Graf. He sent her $185 to buy a necklace to wear while playing. When Seles replaced Graf as the top-ranked tennis player, Parche was crushed. He quit his job. He even said he lost his will to live. By stabbing Seles, Parche hoped to remove her from competition so that Graf would be ranked number one again.

Sadly, his plan worked. It was two years—not two weeks—before Monica Seles could play tennis again. And Graf did regain the number-one ranking. The attack shook up the tennis world. Officials tightened security at matches. They made sure no fan could sneak up behind a player. Still, there was no way they could stop lunatics from falling in love with tennis stars.

In 1999, Dubravko Rajcevic saw Martina Hingis playing tennis on TV. At the time, she was the top female player in the world. Rajcevic became obsessed with Hingis. He sent her love letters. He sent flowers to her home. Rajcevic even began to follow Hingis as she toured the world playing tennis.

Rajcevic never threatened Hingis. He never carried a gun or a knife. But his constant presence scared her. And in light of what had happened to Seles, Hingis could never be sure what this man might do next. Hingis said he was "frightening at times."

Hingis' friends told Rajcevic to stay away. But he would not listen. For some reason, he thought Hingis was *in love with him*. So he hung around outside her home, hoping to see her.

At last, in June 1999, Hingis came out and spoke to Rajcevic. This was the only time she dealt with him face to face. "I told him he should get out of my life," recalled Hingis. "I didn't want to talk with him anymore. I wouldn't want to spend any time with him. I told him he should go away."

But Rajcevic kept stalking her. In 2000, the police arrested him in Miami, where Hingis was playing in a tournament. The police charged Rajcevic with three counts of trespassing and one count of stalking. But he was released from jail after posting $1,000 bail.

Rajcevic still didn't get the message. Despite warnings to stay away from Hingis, he bought a ticket to her next match. The police arrested him again. This time he was held on a $2 million bond. He didn't have that much money. So he stayed in jail. "This guy is obviously a little strange," said Hingis. "[Maybe he is] a little crazy."

Psychologists examined Rajcevic. They said he suffered from delusions. Rajcevic protested. "I am not delusional," he said. "I am not mentally ill."

Sick or not, the court ruled that Rajcevic was competent to stand trial. He faced up to four years in prison. At his trial, he maintained that he wasn't "stalking" Hingis. He was just "wooing" her. "Is it wrong," he asked, "if I want to marry Martina?" Being around her, he said, was "an expression of love." He added, "I thought Martina could be the lady in my life."

The jury didn't buy his story. They found Rajcevic guilty. He was sentenced to two years in prison. By then, he had already spent a year in jail. So he only had to serve one more year. He didn't think he deserved any jail time at all. "I'm not happy," he told the judge.

Rajcevic had to promise he would never bother Hingis again. He couldn't have any contact with her or her family or her manager. He agreed to sign a court order promising to stay away from Hingis for 150 years!

Someone asked Rajcevic if he thought Hingis ever loved him. "Yes, I believe she was in love with me, but I've been in jail for one year," he said. "She's young, beautiful, famous. In one year she's probably found someone else." He added, "I am not interested anymore in Martina Hingis because she turned her back on me. She lied in [the] courtroom."

As for Martina Hingis, she was just happy it was over. "I'm definitely very, very happy that I don't have to think about it anymore," she said. "I went through it, and now it's over."

If you have been timed while reading this article, enter your reading time below. Then turn to the Words-per-Minute Table on page 120 and look up your reading speed (words per minute). Enter your reading speed on the graph on page 121.

**Reading Time:** Selection 2

_____ : _____
MINUTES     SECONDS

**UNDERSTANDING IDEAS** Circle the letter of the best answer.

1. **Why did Guenter Parche stab Monica Seles?**
   A  He wanted to kill her.
   B  He wanted her to beat Steffi Graf.
   C  He wanted to stop her from playing tennis for a while.
   D  He wanted to win the tennis match.

2. **Dubravko Rajcevic stalked Martina Hingis because**
   F  he loved tennis
   G  he wanted to marry her
   H  he wanted Steffi Graf to beat her
   J  he wanted a ticket to her next match

3. **What did Hingis tell Rajcevic?**
   A  She told him that she loved him.
   B  She told him he should go away.
   C  She told him how to improve his game.
   D  She told him that they would marry when he got out of jail.

4. **At his trial, Rajcevic told the court that**
   F  he had been ignoring Hingis
   G  he had been in jail
   H  he had been acting out of love
   J  he had been stalking Hingis

**SUMMARIZE** For each blank, choose the word that best completes the meaning of the paragraph.

| hurt | win | kill |
|------|-----|------|
| jail | tennis | stalking |

Guenter Parche did not want to _____ Monica Seles. He only wanted to _____ her so she wouldn't be able to play tennis for a while. Parche was in love with Steffi Graf. He wanted to make sure that Graf would _____ over Seles. Dubravko Rajcevic was in love with another _____ player. He got arrested for _____ Martina Hingis. Both men ended up in _____. Whoever thought tennis was a game of love?

**IF YOU WERE THERE** Imagine you were a member of the jury that found Rajcevic guilty. Write a brief paragraph explaining your reasons. Be sure to include examples from the story to support your response.

_____
_____
_____
_____
_____

**USE CONTEXT CLUES** When you read, you may find a word whose meaning is unfamiliar to you. When that happens, you can look up the word's meaning in the dictionary. You can also find out what the word means by looking for context clues. These are words or sentences that come before or after the word. Context clues can be antonyms or synonyms of the unfamiliar word. They may also be an example or definition of the unfamiliar word.

Read each excerpt from the stories you just read. Circle the letter with the best meaning of the underlined word.

1. **Everyone agreed that the man wasn't a robber. Cash and credit cards, which were clearly visible, had not been touched.**
   A  hidden, tucked away
   B  important
   C  in full view, able to be seen
   D  worth a lot of money

2. **Flatley also took other measures which he refused to reveal. . . . Flatley wanted the man to know he had beefed up his security, but he didn't want to give away all the details.**
   F  make known
   G  recall
   H  remember
   J  pay for

3. **Flatley tried to keep a low profile in his personal life. "I've spent more money trying to stay out of the papers than most stars spend trying to get into them," he said.**
   A  sense of humor
   B  level of public display
   C  amount of money
   D  level of anger

4. **Overzealous fans follow stars wherever they go. The worst of these fans become stalkers.**
   F  obviously angry
   G  funny
   H  very enthusiastic
   J  happy

5. **Rajcevic never threatened Hingis. He never carried a gun or knife.**
   A  spoke to
   B  endangered or harmed
   C  doubted
   D  stabbed

**PUT WORDS INTO CONTEXT** Complete the paragraph using the underlined words from the exercise on this page.

Most celebrities do not like to

_____ details about their private

lives. Yet some of these details are highly

_____. Celebrity papers publish

stories and pictures that _____

fans love to read. But some fans go too far. Celebrity

stalkers have _____ the security of

many stars and their families. Sometimes, sending

stalkers to jail is the only way to stop them.

**ANTONYMS** An antonym is a word that has the opposite meaning of another word. For example, *remember* is an antonym for the word *forget*.

Circle the letter of the word or phrase that means the OPPOSITE of the underlined word or words.

1. **"The image and fear of that moment has stuck with me and left me frightened, mad, and <u>vulnerable</u>."**
   A protected
   B disappointed
   C surprised
   D terrified

2. **These fans become so <u>obsessed</u> that they want to share the personal lives of their heroes.**
   F involved
   G confused
   H uninvolved
   J lonely

3. **"It's a <u>disgrace</u> that people can do this kind of thing.**
   A reason
   B honor
   C sure thing
   D pity

4. **It turned out that Parche was in love with one of Monica's <u>rivals</u>, Steffi Graf.**
   F players
   G enemies
   H friends
   J opponents

5. **Rajcevic had a <u>delusion</u> that Martina Hingis was in love with him.**
   A loneliness
   B false beliefs
   C injuries
   D a belief that is true

**ANTONYM ANALOGIES** Analogies show similar patterns between words. Antonym analogies show patterns between words that have opposite meanings. For example, *large* is to *small* as *tall* is to *short*. For each blank, choose an underlined word from the exercise on this page to correctly complete the analogy.

1. *Opponents* is to *teammates* as

   _____ is to *friends*.

2. *Fantasy* is to *fact* as

   _____ is to *reality*.

3. *Open* is to *closed* as

   _____ is to *safe*.

4. *Riches* is to *poverty* as

   _____ is to *honor*.

5. *Worried* is to *relaxed* as

   _____ is to *unconcerned*.

**ORGANIZE THE FACTS** A summary retells the major points of a story. Minor details and examples are not included. To write a summary, first you must decide what the most important points are. You can do this by making a list. Then write a paragraph using the main points from your list. The paragraph is your summary.

Look at the major points listed under "Mad With Fear." Fill in the missing information. Then list the major points of "Tennis Love."

| "Mad with Fear" |
|---|
| 1. Like many other celebrities, Michael Flatley worried about fans invading his privacy. |
| 2. A stalker managed to get by his guards and enter his home. |
| 3. Flatley was unharmed but very shaken by the incident. |
| 4. |
| 5. He added more security measures to his home. |

| "Tennis Love" |
|---|
| 1. In April of 1993, Guenter Parche stabbed Monica Seles. |
| 2. |
| 3. |
| 4. |
| 5. |

**SUMMARIZE THE STORY** Using the major points listed above, write a brief paragraph summarizing "Tennis Love."

_____

_____

_____

_____

_____

_____

## MAKE INFERENCES

An author doesn't always state an idea directly in a passage, but you can determine what it is by applying your own knowledge and experiences. You can also examine the evidence presented in the text. This is called making an inference. Circle the letter of the best answer.

1. **What can the reader infer from the following sentences?**

   > "He stared straight at me. The hairs shot up on the back of my neck."

   A Flatley had expected to see the man.

   B Flatley was very frightened.

   C Flatley thought he was having a bad dream.

   D Flatley was feeling comfortable.

2. **Which is the best inference a reader can make about the following statement Rajcevic made?**

   > "I am not interested anymore in Martina Hingis because she turned her back on me. She lied in [the] courtroom."

   F Rajcevic was still suffering from delusions.

   G Rajcevic had good reason to be angry at Hingis.

   H Hingis persuaded Rajcevic to leave her alone.

   J Rajcevic is capable of leading a normal life.

3. **What is the best inference a reader can make about the following statement Hingis made?**

   > "I went through it, and now it's over."

   A Hingis will never recover from her experience.

   B Hingis is sorry she pressed charges.

   C Hingis will never be bothered by another stalker.

   D Hingis is able to put the experience behind her.

## APPLY WHAT YOU KNOW

1. **What do you think most readers will feel after reading both stories?**

   A Readers will feel sympathy for celebrity stalkers.

   B Readers will feel sympathy for celebrities.

   C Readers will feel disgusted with themselves.

   D Readers will feel that celebrities are overreacting.

2. **What reason do you think the author might have had for writing the stories?**

   F The author wanted to scare people.

   G The author wanted to write about a serious issue.

   H The author wanted to make fun of celebrities.

   J The author wanted to show dislike for big stars.

## JUDGE THE EVIDENCE

Based on what you have read about stalkers, do you think they only bother famous people? Write a brief paragraph expressing your opinion. Support your opinion with evidence from the stories you have read in this unit.

_____

_____

_____

_____

_____

_____

_____

_____

# DEADLY SPORTS

## Between a Rock and a Hard Place

This was supposed to be an easy climb. Twenty-two-year-old Peter Terbush did not think it would be much of a challenge. Neither did twenty-year-old Kerry Pyle or twenty-one-year-old Joe Kewin. These three men were students at Western State College in Colorado. They were also experienced rock climbers. In fact, they all taught rock climbing classes there. On June 13, 1999, they were in California's Yosemite National Park. Early that morning they set out on what they thought would be a routine climb.

Their plan was to go up Apron Jam Route. It was on the western shoulder of a rock formation called Glacier Point. The climb was only three hundred feet. And the slope of the climb wasn't hard. "That area has great, easy climbing," said Dave Bengston, director of the Yosemite Mountaineering School. "Beginners love to go there because the climb is not real steep." For skilled climbers such as Terbush, Pyle, and Kewin, it was little more than a practice session. They figured they could be up and down in thirty minutes.

The climbing that day *was* easy. But there were hidden dangers. If the three climbers had asked Bengston about the conditions that morning, he would have warned them not to go. The Apron Jam Route is risky in the spring. When the high mountain snow melts, the water often runs into the cracks on Glacier Point. At night, this water freezes. Water expands as it freezes, and the pressure of the ice loosens rocks. "It's a big-time helmet zone," said Bengston. By that he meant that climbers needed helmets to protect their heads from falling rocks. He said, "I hear rocks coming down all the time."

Terbush, Pyle, and Kewin made a mistake by not checking with park officials before they climbed. Rock climbers should always find out what local experts know. That will keep them from taking unnecessary chances. The climb itself is risky enough. Other risks should be reduced to nearly zero. As rock climber Dylan Morgan puts it, "[A] thousand things can go wrong when you're up there."

Terbush, Pyle, and Kewin were not thinking about dangers, however. They were looking forward to a quick and easy outing. By 7:30 A.M., they were at the climbing site. Soon they expected to be at the top of Glacier Point. There they would enjoy a wonderful view of Yosemite Valley three thousand feet below.

Pyle was the lead climber this time, so Terbush and Kewin stood at the bottom while he began his ascent. Terbush held the belay, or safety rope, for him. "It was a famous climb," said Kewin later. "It had some of the best cracks in the valley." Kewin also noted that there were fresh chalk marks on the rocks. That showed that other climbers had gone up recently.

But at 7:35 A.M., a loud sound ripped through the valley. Jerry Bickford, a front desk clerk at the nearby Curry Village Lodge, heard the roar. He rushed outside to see what was happening. All he could see was a cloud of dust. "The first thing that goes through your mind is that it's thunder," Bickford said. "But then the sky is blue so you know it's not that."

Indeed, it wasn't thunder. It was a huge rockslide. Pyle was about seventy feet up when it occurred. It started with small rocks. Then larger rocks began to fall. Eyewitnesses described these rocks as the size of small cars. Abbie Kealey was on top of Glacier Point at the time. "It was like a huge rumbling sound, like a jet coming close," she said. She walked to the edge of the cliff and looked below. "We saw a tiny plume of impact that rose up like a nuclear blast."

The falling boulders missed Pyle. But they were headed right toward Kewin and Terbush. Kewin quickly jumped out of the way. Terbush, however, didn't move. He was holding the safety rope. He had enough time to save himself, but to do so he would have had to let go of the rope. "If he had run," said Pyle later, "he probably would have ripped me off the rock and killed me." And so, although he must have been terrified, Terbush stood his ground. He kept a firm grip on the safety line.

Seconds later, the huge rocks rained down on Peter Terbush, crushing him to death. He had made the ultimate sacrifice. He had given up his life to save the life of a fellow climber. Kewin and others called him a hero. They were right. When rescuers recovered Terbush's body, they saw the rope still firmly in his hands.

If you have been timed while reading this article, enter your reading time below. Then turn to the Words-per-Minute Table on page 120 and look up your reading speed (words per minute). Enter your reading speed on the graph on page 121.

**Reading Time:** Selection 1

_____ : _____
MINUTES        SECONDS

**UNDERSTANDING IDEAS** Circle the letter of the best answer.

**1. Which statement belongs in the empty box?**

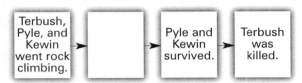

Terbush, Pyle, and Kewin went rock climbing. → [ ] → Pyle and Kewin survived. → Terbush was killed.

    **A** The three men taught rock climbing classes.

    **B** Terbush is called a hero.

    **C** There was a rockslide.

    **D** They spoke with other climbers.

**2. The three men had expected that their climb would be**

    **F** dangerous

    **G** easy

    **H** long

    **J** difficult

**3. If the men had spoken to park officials before the climb, they probably**

    **A** would have made the climb anyway

    **B** would have taken better helmets

    **C** would have taken their time

    **D** wouldn't have made the climb

**4. The loud sound that ripped through the valley that morning was**

    **F** heavy rain

    **G** falling rocks

    **H** thunder

    **J** people calling for help

**5. Because Terbush did not move during the rockslide,**

    **A** he avoided death

    **B** he saved his friend's life

    **C** he dropped the safety rope

    **D** he was thrown down the slope

**SUMMARIZE** For each blank, choose the word that best completes the meaning of the paragraph.

| safety | life | dangerous |
|---|---|---|
| climb | crushed | fall |

The three young men thought the

_____ would be routine. Instead,

it proved to be very _____.

In the end, Peter Terbush died. He was holding

the _____ rope. Huge rocks

_____ him as he held onto the rope.

He gave up his _____ to protect his

friend from a deadly _____.

**IF YOU WERE THERE** What would you have done if you had been in Peter Terbush's place? Write a brief paragraph explaining your actions. Be sure to include examples from the story to support your response.

_____

_____

_____

_____

_____

_____

# Hell on Highwater

It was Kristy McAlister's first sea rescue, and she was scared to death. "I was petrified," she later said. McAlister was a paramedic with the SouthCare ambulance helicopter. On December 27, 1998, she was called out over the harsh waters of the Bass Strait. Sailors were in trouble there. She had to help rescue them before they drowned.

The day before, 115 yachts had set sail from Sydney, Australia. They were all headed for Hobart, Tasmania. This 724-mile-race across the Bass Strait was called "Hell on Highwater." It had been given that nickname because the strait could be very rough. Still, in the race's 54-year-history, only two sailors had died.

The weather forecast on December 26 had called for a storm to develop. There was a chance of high winds and rough seas. Still, race officials had decided to go ahead with the race. More than 300,000 fans had packed Sydney Harbor to see the start. And at the time the yachts took off, the sky was blue and clear. There wasn't a cloud in sight. One sailor described the conditions as "magic."

The "magic" soon turned to terror. By the next day a powerful storm had moved into the Bass Strait. It was even stronger than the forecasters had expected. Weather experts had predicted winds of up to 55 miles an hour. That would have been bad enough. But these winds shrieked at 90 miles an hour! They kicked up waves more than 60 feet high.

The fastest yachts passed through the treacherous Bass Strait before the full fury of the storm struck. But the slower boats were there to take the brunt of it. The winds and waves tossed the boats around like bath toys. Masts snapped in half. Dozens of sailors got washed overboard. One wave swept Glyn Charles over the side of the *Sword of Orion*. His mates tried to save him. But the winds and waves were too rough. Within minutes, Charles was gone.

Peter Joubert, age seventy-four, had sailed in twenty-seven Sydney-to-Hobart races. But he had never seen anything like this. "It was an absolute maelstrom," he said, "like a scene from hell."

Melissa McCabe, a high school student, had earned a spot on one of the yachts by winning a writing contest. "People were getting sick," she later said. "When the wave hit, the deck above me cracked. It was like a waterfall in the middle of the boat."

The cries of "Mayday! Mayday! Mayday!" filled the radio waves. Rescue helicopters rushed to the scene. Kristy McAlister was in one of them. "There wasn't a lot of visibility and there were 60- to 70-foot waves," she recalled.

"I just looked at the sea and thought, 'Oh, my God.'"

McAlister and other paramedics were lowered into the water on cables. Above them, the pilots struggled to hold the helicopters steady in the high winds. The paramedics' job was to reach floundering sailors and strap them into rescue harnesses. Then helicopter crews could haul the sailors up from the sea. Twice McAlister managed to do this. But it wasn't easy. "Just as I was hitting the water, one of the waves came in, and I was dumped under the water for quite some time," she said. "I didn't panic. [But] I did swallow a fair bit of seawater, which made me quite sick."

Peter Davidson's helicopter was sent to rescue sailors from the *Stand-A-Side*. This boat had been destroyed by the storm. Its mast had broken off. Its cabin had been ripped apart. Its crew were now clinging to a small life raft that was being tossed wildly up and down. Davidson had worked as a rescue paramedic for eight years. But he had never witnessed a scene like this.

"When we arrived at the scene, we were looking at the waves with open mouths," he said. "We were hovering at around 80 feet and there were waves 60 to 70 feet high. I was feeling very apprehensive about that. I just really didn't think I'd be able to save anyone."

Still, Davidson vowed to give it his best shot. After being lowered into the water, he fought his way through the waves. He reached the life raft and strapped a sailor into a harness. Then he did it again. And again. Eight times Davidson went down into the swirling water to save a life. Like McAlister, he was repeatedly buried by the waves. He later admitted, "There were a couple of times where I thought, 'This is it. My number's up!'"

On his final rescue, a fierce wind drove him deep under the water. "It was as though I was hit by an almighty explosion," he said. "As I placed the [harness] around the eighth yachtsman, I was so exhausted I could barely muster the energy to give the thumbs-up signal."

In all, rescuers managed to pull more than fifty sailors out of the sea. But a total of six sailors drowned in the storm. Of the 115 boats that began the race, only 39 finished it. Six boats sank. The rest sailed to the nearest land. If any doubters had questioned the race's nickname before, they didn't question it anymore. The Sydney-to-Hobart yacht race really was "Hell on Highwater."

If you have been timed while reading this article, enter your reading time below. Then turn to the Words-per-Minute Table on page 120 and look up your reading speed (words per minute). Enter your reading speed on the graph on page 121.

**Reading Time:** Selection 2

_____ : _____
MINUTES     SECONDS

**UNDERSTANDING IDEAS** Circle the letter of the best answer.

1. **When the Sydney-to-Hobart yacht race began, the weather was**

   A clear

   B cloudy

   C very warm

   D very windy

2. **The slower yachts were hardest hit by the storm because**

   F they weren't built as well as the faster yachts

   G they were in the rough Bass Strait when the storm hit

   H the faster yachts waited before passing through the strait

   J these yachts pulled out of the race

3. **Paramedics and rescue crews saved sailors by**

   A strapping them to their backs

   B pulling them into safety rafts

   C hauling them up into helicopters

   D throwing them life jackets

4. **Why was the yacht race nicknamed "Hell on Highwater"?**

   F Many sailors drown each year.

   G Only a few yachts finish the race.

   H The strait was known to be rough.

   J The waves at that time of year are very high.

**SUMMARIZE** For each blank, choose the word that best completes the meaning of the paragraph.

| storm | helicopters | nickname |
|---|---|---|
| sailors | yacht | waves |

On December 27, 1998, the Sydney-to-Hobart

_____ race earned its

_____, "Hell on Highwater." A

powerful _____ blew into the Bass

Strait. Winds and high _____

broke boats apart and threw _____

overboard. Paramedics were flown in on

_____ to rescue the sailors.

They risked their own lives and were able to save

more than 50 sailors.

**IF YOU WERE THERE** Write a brief paragraph explaining what you would have done if you had been in the race that day. Be sure to include examples from the story to support your response.

_____

_____

_____

_____

_____

_____

**USE CONTEXT CLUES** When you read, you may find a word whose meaning is unfamiliar to you. When that happens, you can look up the word's meaning in the dictionary. You can also find out what the word means by looking for context clues. These are words or sentences that come before or after the word. Context clues can be antonyms or synonyms of the unfamiliar word. They may also be an example or definition of the unfamiliar word.

Read each excerpt from the stories you just read. Circle the letter with the best meaning of the underlined word.

1. **This was supposed to be an easy climb. Twenty-two-year-old Peter Terbush did not think it would be much of a challenge.**

   A sport

   B good time

   C difficult thing to do

   D steep slope

2. **On December 27, 1998, she was called out over the harsh waters of the Bass Strait. Sailors were in trouble there.**

   F slightly moving

   G cold but calm

   H unpleasantly rough

   J bitter and salty

3. **"I was feeling very apprehensive about that. I just really didn't think I'd be able to save anyone."**

   A crazy, wild

   B tired

   C lively

   D cautious, worried

4. **He had made the ultimate sacrifice. He had given up his life to save the life of a fellow climber.**

   F a surprising gift to a friend

   G something given up voluntarily

   H punishment

   J correction

5. **It was even stronger than the forecasters had expected. . . . Weather experts had predicted winds up to 55 miles an hour.**

   A weather reporters

   B storytellers

   C those who must go outside in bad weather

   D people who like to go outside

**PUT WORDS INTO CONTEXT** Complete the paragraph using the underlined words from the exercise on this page.

Few sports are deadly, but all can present an

unexpected _____. For those

who prefer water sports, storms can create

_____ conditions at a moment's

notice. Participating in a dangerous sport may cause

one to feel _____, especially

during bad weather. Make sure to check with weather

_____ before you start.

## SIMILES, METAPHORS, AND PERSONIFICATION

Writers use similes, metaphors, and personification to make their writing more vivid. Similes and metaphors are comparisons between words. Similes are easy to spot because they are preceded by the words *like* or *as*. Here is an example: *She was as tall as a tree*. Here is another simile: *Ben is tall like a tree*. Metaphors are comparisons that do not use the words *like* or *as*. For example: *Daryl was a tiger on the court*. The sentence means that Daryl was a strong, powerful player. When writers use personification, they give inanimate objects human qualities. For example: *The wind moaned and howled*.

Read the following sentences. Write S for simile, M for metaphor, or P for personification in the blank on the left.

_____ **1.** The winds and waves tossed the boats around like bath toys.

_____ **2.** The angry, vengeful storm attacked the yachts.

_____ **3.** The waves around the crew of the *Stand-A-Side* were massive explosions.

_____ **4.** The rocks rolled down Glacier Point like a wild stampede of cattle.

_____ **5.** The brave, courageous yacht fought the storm as long as it could before sinking.

## WHAT'S THE COMPARISON?

Read the following sentences. In the space provided, write what two things are being compared.

**1.** The rocks were like small cars.

_____

**2.** The wind tore through the boat like a sharp knife.

_____

**3.** The sailors felt fear like a hand wrapped around their throats. _____

**4.** The helicopter cables swung like threads.

_____

**5.** The waves were as tall as skyscrapers.

_____

**ORGANIZE THE FACTS** There are several different ways to organize your writing. In stories like the ones you just read, the sequence, or order, of the events is very important. In the charts below, fill in the next event(s) in the order that they happened.

| "Between a Rock and a Hard Place" |
| --- |
| 1. On June 13, 1999, Terbush, Pyle, and Kewin went to California's Yosemite National Park. |
| 2. They decided to go up Apron Jam Route for an easy climb. |
| 3. By 7:30 A.M., they were at the climbing site. |
| 4. By 7:35 A.M., a loud sound ripped through the valley. It was a rockslide! |
| 5. |

| "Hell on Highwater" |
| --- |
| 1. On December 27, 1998, the annual Sydney-to-Hobart yacht race began. |
| 2. |
| 3. |
| 4. |
| 5. |

**PUT DETAILS IN SEQUENCE** Choose the best answer for each question.

1. **When did the following happen? Where should it be in the sequence chart about "Between a Rock and a Hard Place"?**

   | A falling boulder misses Pyle. |
   | --- |

   **A** before 1

   **B** between 1 and 2

   **C** between 2 and 3

   **D** after 4

2. **In the chart named "Hell on Highwater," where would you place the information about Peter Davidson's rescue mission?**

   **F** at the beginning of the chart

   **G** in the middle of the chart

   **H** toward the end of the chart

   **J** nowhere on the chart

**MAKE INFERENCES** Inferences are what the reader learns from what the writer has written. When you make an inference, you consider the evidence you've read and then decide what the message is, if it has not already been clearly stated. Circle the letter of the best answer.

1. **What can the reader infer from the following paragraph?**

   > The cries of "Mayday! Mayday! Mayday!" filled the radio waves. Rescue helicopters rushed to the scene. Kristy McAlister was in one of them. "There wasn't a lot of visibility and there were 60 to 70 foot waves," she recalled. "I just looked at the sea and thought, 'Oh, my God.'"

   A Kristy didn't think the sailors really needed help.

   B Kristy had a clear view of the area.

   C Kristy feared that many lives would be lost.

   D Kristy will decide not to leave the helicopter.

2. **Which is the best inference a reader can make about these sentences?**

   > After being lowered into the water, he fought his way through the waves. He reached the life raft and strapped a sailor into a harness. Then he did it again. And again.

   F Peter Davidson was a very determined man.

   G Davidson couldn't strap the sailor into the harness.

   H Davidson was losing hope.

   J Davidson would surely die.

**APPLY WHAT YOU KNOW** Choose the best answer.

1. **Why do you think the author chose "Hell on Highwater" for the title of this selection?**

   A to create a sense of drama

   B to give the yacht race a new name

   C to show that racing is not dangerous

   D to explain a boating term

2. **By saying that "The Sydney-to-Hobart yacht race really was 'Hell on Highwater,'" the author wanted to**

   F tell readers to stay out of the water

   G show that the race had a fitting nickname

   H make officials cancel all future races

   J confuse the reader

**JUDGE THE EVIDENCE** Based on the two stories, do you think heroes have qualities that set them apart from other people, or do you think circumstances create heroes out of ordinary people? Write a brief paragraph stating what you believe. Support your opinion with evidence from the stories.

## The Ghost of Humpty Doo

The trouble started when Kirsty and Andrew Agius came to town. They and their eleven-month-old daughter Jasmine moved into a four-bedroom home with three friends. The group shared the rent and the upkeep of the five-acre spread just south of Humpty Doo, Australia. But their happy existence didn't last long. Soon after Kirsty and her family arrived, an unwanted visitor shattered the peace and quiet.

It happened in February of 1998. Kirsty, Andrew, and their friends were sitting out on the porch. A thunderstorm had just passed through. Night was falling. Suddenly, from out of nowhere, small pebbles began to rain down on them. At first the group thought someone was playing a joke. So they moved inside. But so did the pebbles! Handfuls of half-inch stones fell all over the floor. Some landed on tables. Some landed on beds. The pebbles looked as if they might have come from the gravel driveway. But the stones in the driveway were still wet from the recent rain. The pebbles falling inside were bone dry.

Other objects began to fly around the house. Kirsty and Andrew saw batteries whiz through the air. They found a steak knife stuck into their bed. They saw a piece of soap come out of the wall and fly toward a ceiling fan. Kirsty and Andrew were terrified. And their problems were not over yet.

Next they found messages spelled out with pebbles. Messages also appeared in letters from a Scrabble game. The messages were short and spooky. They came as a series of single words. Among these were the words FIRE, SKIN, CAR, HELP and TROY. Kirsty and Andrew couldn't believe it. A month earlier, a good friend named Troy had been killed in a fiery car crash. Were these messages about him? What did they mean?

Completely unnerved, they called in a priest. Father Tom English came to the house. As he walked in, a bullet dropped from the air. It fell right at his feet. A bottle also flew from an empty room. When Father Tom tried to pray, glass broke all over the house. Windows shattered. The priest's Bible was hurled through the air.

"I have never seen anything like it before," said Father Tom.

Neither had local reporters. They soon heard that a poltergeist was in the Humpty Doo house. "Poltergeist" is a German word. It means "noisy ghost." A TV show called *ABC Midday* did an interview with Father Tom. Another show, *Today Tonight*, sent a camera crew to the house. Six different journalists also came. So did a "ghostbuster" named Steve Bishop.

The *Today Tonight* crew concluded that the story was a hoax. They thought Kirsty was behind it all. Their cameras did capture an object flying through the air. But a closer look at the film showed a shadowy figure in the background. It was Kirsty. Her image was being reflected in a glass cabinet. The TV crew believed this proved that she was faking the whole thing.

Others disagreed. They thought something paranormal really was happening. For one thing, they doubted that Kirsty would endanger her own child by throwing pebbles, knives, and glass all over the place. Besides, these other reporters saw for themselves many of the weird things that Kirsty had described. They saw bottles fly across the room. They saw bullets, knives, and stones fall from thin air. Reporter Nikki Voss had her back to a solid wall when pebbles began to pelt her in the neck. Tracey Farrar saw a piece of her radio equipment rise up off a table. Writer Tony Healy saw a small brass ball drop onto the table in front of him. Kirsty was sitting at the same table with him at the time. She was reading the newspaper, holding it with both hands. To Healy, this proved that "a hoax was almost out

of the question." He and his writing partner, Paul Cropper, said that several of the events they witnessed seemed "unfakeable." Ghostbuster Steve Bishop also believed the events were real. He said there was a "dangerous" force in the house. It was, said Bishop, an "extreme case" of haunting.

For three months, Kirsty and her housemates put up with all the bizarre happenings. But by May, they had had enough. They moved out of the house. With that, the poltergeist seemed to vanish. Did that mean that Kirsty really was fooling everyone? Or did it simply mean that the ghost of Humpty Doo was taking a break, waiting for the next chance to make someone scared stiff?

If you have been timed while reading this article, enter your reading time below. Then turn to the Words-per-Minute Table on page 120 and look up your reading speed (words per minute). Enter your reading speed on the graph on page 121.

**Reading Time:** Selection 1

_____ : _____
MINUTES     SECONDS

## UNDERSTANDING IDEAS Circle the letter of the best answer.

**1. What was the first indication that something was wrong?**

A Objects floated around the house.

B Kirsty and Andrew received spooky messages.

C Pebbles and stones rained down on them.

D A priest made a visit.

**2. Proof that the pebbles had not come from the driveway is that**

F they were different shapes and sizes

G they were dry, but the driveway pebbles were wet

H they followed the people indoors

J they were wet with rain

**3. What made some reporters believe something out of the ordinary was happening?**

A They did not think Australia was a good place for ghosts.

B They had seen ghosts at the house before Kirsty moved in.

C They felt that Kirsty was making up the whole story.

D They saw the same things Kirsty had reported.

**4. Based on the evidence in the story, the reader can conclude that**

F there was no poltergeist

G there was a logical explanation for what happened

H there was no logical explanation for what happened

J there is nothing that a real poltergeist can't do

## SUMMARIZE For each blank, choose the word that best completes the meaning of the paragraph.

| strange | events | crew |
|---------|--------|------|
| fool | ghost | faking |

Did Kirsty Agius really _____ everyone, or did a _____ in their house at Humpty Doo cause objects to fly around the house? A TV _____ from *Today Tonight* thought Kirsty's story was a hoax. They believed that their film had caught Kirsty _____ the whole thing. But a "ghostbuster" and several reporters believed that the _____ were "unfakeable." Whatever the answer, after three months of very _____ happenings, Kirsty Agius and her housemates moved.

## IF YOU WERE THERE Write a brief paragraph explaining what you might do if you were given the chance to live in Kirsty's house for free. Be sure to include examples from the story to support your response.

_____

_____

_____

_____

_____

# A Hoax or a Haunting?

Susan Melbourne and her sister Sandra grew up in Lowes Cottage. It was a quaint little house in Derbyshire, England, and the girls had an idyllic childhood there. They romped in the garden and slept soundly down the hall from their parents. To them, the 300-year-old house was a cozy and inviting place. But the next owners saw things differently. To these people, Lowes Cottage was "a living hell."

In 1993, the Melbourne family sold the house to Andrew and Josie Smith. By then, the house had sat empty for some time. It was quite run down. The Smiths planned to restore it and raise their own children there. They spent a lot of time and money fixing up the place. At last they moved in. For six weeks everything went well. Then Andrew began to get the feeling that someone was watching him. It made him nervous. He felt that the presence was "evil." Josie soon confirmed this impression. She woke up one night and felt something attacking her.

"I felt a heavy weight pressing down on me, and it took every ounce of strength in me just to lift my little finger," she recalled. "Then suddenly it just flew across my face."

Josie and Andrew also noticed a foul smell in the air. "There was a strong, pungent smell around the house and we could find no explanation for it," said Josie. "We thought perhaps it was damp because the house hadn't been lived in for so long."

The Smiths made some inquiries around town. What they found shocked and upset them. According to legend, two people had died horrible deaths in the house. In the 1600s, a maid had died locked in the cellar. Years later, a young boy had hanged himself in one of the rooms. The Smiths began to wonder if the ghosts of these people were haunting Lowes Cottage.

Every day, it seemed, something new and unsettling happened. The temperature in various rooms dropped suddenly. Floorboards creaked as though someone was walking past. The walls began to drip with slime. "Twice I felt as if I was being strangled," said Josie, "and I woke up choking and shaking. Both times we had to leave the house. It was gripping me round the throat and throttling me. My whole body was shaking. I thought I was doing to die."

"I was a total cynic about such things," Andrew said. "I didn't believe in the supernatural. But not anymore. We are genuinely terrified."

The Smiths called in a priest. Reverend Peter Mockford did his best. He tried several times to bless the house, but it didn't help. The bizarre events continued. The priest came away convinced that the Smiths were right: there was something evil in the house. "I myself experienced the smell and the wet walls," Mockford said. He described the smell as "unbelievably vile. Truly foul. You would be hard-pressed to manufacture something of that line, particularly something that comes and goes. If it was there all the time you could say it was a dead cat under the floorboards. But it was not localized, and it tended to move around." Mockford summed up his thoughts by saying, "In my view, in Lowes Cottage there is paranormal activity which cannot be explained."

At last, they couldn't take it any longer. They decided to sell the house. But a real estate agent told them its value had dropped because of all the strange occurrences. Feeling desperate, the Smiths decided to sue the people who had sold them the house. They argued that the Melbournes should have told them about the ghosts. Lawyer Stephen Savage said, "It's the same as if the [sellers] did not declare faulty central heating or drains. If the Smiths had known about the cottage's history they would not have bought it. The fact is that the property has quite a reputation locally and this was not disclosed."

"We want only one thing, to get away from [the house]," said Josie. "And the court action is our only chance of recouping our capital."

The Melbourne sisters were outraged by the lawsuit. "It's all a load of rubbish," said Susan Melbourne. "I grew up in Lowes Cottage and nothing strange happened to me at all. I've never heard of the cottage having such a reputation."

Judge Peter Stratton agreed with the Melbournes. He noted that the Smiths had tried to make money by charging admission to a Halloween party they held in the house. He also noted that they had both read *The Amityville Horror*, a book that detailed the similar haunting of a house in Amityville, New York. He pointed out that the Smiths were claiming to experience exactly the same things the Amityville couple had experienced. In short, the judge didn't believe them. He didn't believe Lowes Cottage contained ghosts. "This house is not haunted and has never been haunted," he declared.

Defeated, the Smiths decided to walk away from their troubles, letting the bank take possession of the house. In 2000, a man named Tim Chilton bought the house at a bank auction. He didn't know if he would have any encounters with ghosts; he said he would just have to wait and see. "It doesn't feel like a story ending," he told one reporter. "It feels like a story beginning."

If you have been timed while reading this article, enter your reading time below. Then turn to the Words-per-Minute Table on page 120 and look up your reading speed (words per minute). Enter your reading speed on the graph on page 121.

**Reading Time:** Selection 2

_____ : _____
MINUTES       SECONDS

**UNDERSTANDING IDEAS** Circle the letter of the best answer.

1. **Why did the Smiths sue the Melbournes?**
   A They thought that the Melbournes should have told them about the ghosts.
   B They thought the Melbournes were responsible for repairs.
   C They wanted the Melbournes to get rid of the ghosts.
   D They thought the Melbournes were trying to scare them away.

2. **What was the judge's ruling in the lawsuit?**
   F The judge ruled in favor of the Melbournes.
   G The judge ruled that the house was, in fact, haunted.
   H The judge ruled in favor of the Smiths.
   J The judge allowed a jury to rule on the case.

3. **The Melbourne sisters strongly objected to the Smith's lawsuit because**
   A a deal is a deal
   B they denied that strange things had ever happened
   C they felt the lawsuit would give the house a bad reputation
   D they thought the Smiths had lowered the value of the property

4. **What was one reason the judge gave for the outcome of the lawsuit?**
   F Tim Chilton was willing to live in the house.
   G The Smiths seemed to have had the same experiences as the characters in a popular book.
   H the testimony of Reverend Mockford
   J the good reputation of the Melbourne sisters

**SUMMARIZE** For each blank, choose the word that best completes the meaning of the paragraph.

| agree | convinced | events |
|---|---|---|
| odor | attacked | haunted |

Even though Reverend Peter Mockford came away _____ that there was some evil in Lowes Cottage, Judge Peter Stratton decided that the house was not _____. There was a very foul _____ that filled the house. Josie awoke one night feeling that she was being _____. All of these _____ had been detailed in *The Amityville Horror*, a book about a haunting in upstate New York. The Smiths did not _____ with the judge's verdict.

**IF YOU WERE THERE** Write a brief paragraph explaining what you would do if you had the Smiths' problem or one like it. Be sure to include examples from the story to support your response.

_____

_____

_____

_____

_____

_____

**USE CONTEXT CLUES** When you read, you may find a word whose meaning is unfamiliar to you. When that happens, you can find its meaning in a dictionary. You can also find out what the word means by looking for context clues. These are words or sentences that come before or after the word. Context clues can be antonyms or synonyms of the unfamiliar word. They may also be an example or definition of the unfamiliar word.

Read each excerpt from the stories you just read. Circle the letter of the best meaning of the underlined word.

1. **It was a quaint little house in Derbyshire, England, and the girls had an idyllic childhood there. They romped in the garden and slept soundly down the hall from their parents. To them, the 300-year-old house was a cozy and inviting place.**

   **A** unpleasant

   **B** boring

   **C** happy and peaceful

   **D** deeply troubling

2. **They thought something paranormal really was happening. . . . Besides, these other reporters saw for themselves the many weird things that Kirsty had described.**

   **F** supernatural

   **G** typical

   **H** dishonest

   **J** mental

3. **He described the smell as "unbelievably vile. Truly foul."**

   **A** dead

   **B** weak

   **C** unpleasant

   **D** friendly

4. **If the Smiths had known about the cottage's history, they would not have bought it. The fact is that the property has quite a reputation locally and this was not disclosed.**

   **F** hidden

   **G** made known, revealed

   **H** taken seriously

   **J** laughed about

5. **"I was a total cynic about such things," Andrew said, "I didn't believe in the supernatural."**

   **A** person who accepts what he is told

   **B** person who raises doubts

   **C** stubborn person

   **D** uncaring person

---

**PUT WORDS INTO CONTEXT** Complete the paragraph using the underlined words from the exercise on this page.

When people report _____

occurrences, a _____ will assume

their stories are made-up. Yet there seems to

be no logical explanation for some of the events that are

_____ by the victims. Why would

anyone *choose* to have a haunting experience over an

_____ one?

**PREFIXES** A prefix is one or more letters added to the beginning of a word to change its meaning. For example, the prefix *para-* means "beyond." The word *paranormal* means "outside of the normal" or "that which cannot be explained scientifically." The prefix *un-* means "not." When you add the prefix *un-* to the beginning of the word *usual*, you get *unusual*, which means "something that is not usual."

Use a dictionary to find the meaning of each prefix below. Match the prefix with its meaning on the right. Examples for each definition are included in italics. Write the letter of the correct definition on the line. **One of the letters will be used twice.**

| | | | |
|---|---|---|---|
| _____ | **1.** mis- | **A** | do the opposite of, not: *unavailable, disappear* |
| _____ | **2.** un- | | |
| _____ | **3.** re- | **B** | the part in the middle: *midsummer* |
| _____ | **4.** dis- | **C** | badly, wrongly: *misunderstood* |
| _____ | **5.** mid- | | |
| _____ | **6.** pre- | **D** | again: *reorder* |
| _____ | **7.** anti- | **E** | against: *antitheft* |
| | | **F** | before: *preview* |

**WRITE DEFINITIONS** On the line next to each word from the story, write the new meaning of the word with the added prefix.

**1.** re + claim = reclaim

definition: _____

**2.** pre + pay = prepay

definition: _____

**3.** dis + obey = disobey

definition: _____

**4.** mid + night = midnight

definition: _____

**5.** anti + war = antiwar

definition: _____

**6.** mis + lead = mislead

definition: _____

**7.** un + cover = uncover

definition: _____

**ORGANIZE THE FACTS** The two stories you read in this unit are alike in some ways and different in other ways. A Venn diagram can show how they are alike and different. Look at the Venn diagram below. Then choose the best answer to each question.

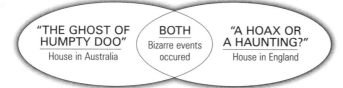

"THE GHOST OF HUMPTY DOO"
House in Australia

BOTH
Bizarre events occured

"A HOAX OR A HAUNTING?"
House in England

1. **Which of the following details belongs in the oval marked BOTH?**

   **A** The people sued the previous owners.

   **B** The events were like those described in *The Amityville Horror*.

   **C** Clergymen were called in to bless the house.

   **D** A TV show sent its crew to the house.

2. **Which detail does NOT belong in the oval marked "The Ghost of Humpty Doo"?**

   **F** The walls dripped with slime.

   **G** Single-word messages appeared.

   **H** Pebbles and stones fell inside the house.

   **J** Radio equipment rose up off a table.

3. **Which detail does NOT belong in the oval marked "A Hoax or a Haunting?"**

   **A** A foul smell filled the house.

   **B** A maid had once died locked in the cellar.

   **C** A Halloween party had been held in the house.

   **D** Objects flew around the house.

**CONTINUE THE COMPARISON** Fill in the chart with additional details about the two stories in this unit.

| More ways the stories are alike: |
|---|
| 1. |
| 2. |
| 3. |
| 4. |

| More ways the stories are different: |
|---|
| 1. |
| 2. |
| 3. |
| 4. |

**FACT AND OPINION** Facts and opinions can sometimes be hard to tell apart. People often represent an opinion as if it were a fact. To tell if something is a fact or an opinion, determine whether what is being said is something that can be proven to be true. If it can, it's a fact. If it states what someone thinks or how someone feels, it's an opinion.

Read this passage about other haunted houses. Then choose the best answer to each question.

[1] Everyone is entertained by movies and books about haunted houses. [2] But when similar events happen in real life, some people become alarmed. [3] Newspapers and TV shows occasionally get reports of hauntings. [4] They should always send reporters to follow up on these leads. [5] Some of these reports, whether proven true or false, come to the public's attention. [6] Most of the stories reported are hoaxes.

**1. Which sentence from the paragraph states a FACT?**

   A  Sentence 1

   B  Sentence 4

   C  Sentence 5

   D  Sentence 6

**2. Which sentence from the paragraph states an OPINION?**

   F  Sentence 2

   G  Sentence 3

   H  Sentence 5

   J  Sentence 6

**JUDGE THE EVIDENCE** Think back to what you have just read. Then choose the best answer.

**1. Which of the following statements is TRUE?**

   A  All reports of haunted houses are true.

   B  Most supernatural experiences cannot be explained.

   C  Everyone has had an experience with a haunted house.

   D  There should be more TV shows about haunted houses.

**2. Which of the following statements is FALSE?**

   F  People are not comfortable in places that appear to be haunted.

   G  Paranormal experiences are generally frightening.

   H  People rarely get used to houses that are haunted.

   J  People never make up stories about ghosts.

**JUST THE FACTS** Fill in the chart below with FACTS from the stories you have just read. Make sure you do not include opinions.

| "The Ghost of Humpty Doo" |
| --- |
|  |
|  |
|  |

| "A Hoax or a Haunting?" |
| --- |
|  |
|  |
|  |

# Trick or Treat

"They're bombing New Jersey!" cried the caller.

"How do you know?" asked police officer John Morrison, who took the phone call at a New York City police station.

"I heard it on the radio," the caller told him.

The caller wasn't lying. The radio *was* reporting bombs dropping in New Jersey. It was a little after 8:00 P.M. on October 30, 1938—Halloween Eve. Many Americans were home listening to the "Mercury Theatre on the Air." The program began with dance music. But after a few moments, the announcer broke in with an urgent bulletin. Strange blue flashes had been spotted on the surface of Mars. The program went back to the music, but a second bulletin was soon issued. It stated that "a huge, flaming object" from space had landed on a farm in Grovers Mill, New Jersey. Officials seemed to think the object might be a meteorite.

Again, the program went back to music. But soon there was yet another interruption. This time the news came from a reporter who had gone to Grovers Mill. He reported that the object wasn't a meteorite. It was a spaceship from Mars! "Ladies and gentlemen," he said, "this is the most terrifying thing I have ever witnessed."

The reporter tried to describe the creatures emerging from the spaceship. "Good heaven's, something's wriggling out of the shadow like a gray snake," he cried. "Now it's another one, and another. They look like tentacles to me. There, I can see the thing's body. It's as large as a bear and it glistens like wet leather. But that face. It . . . it's indescribable."

The news got worse. The creatures from Mars quickly wiped out the New Jersey militia. Then they crushed the Army and the Air Force. The Martians blasted everything in their way with a deadly heat-ray. The Martians crossed the Hudson River into New York City, spreading poison gas in all directions. Nothing could stop them.

This was shocking news, to say the least. But it wasn't true. Listeners who had caught the beginning of the radio show knew that. At 8:00 P.M., an announcer had told listeners that they were about to hear a radio play. It was a drama based on an H.G. Wells novel titled *The War of the Worlds*.

Unfortunately, many people missed this introduction. And there were no other explanations until forty minutes later. By then, it was too late. Thousands of people who tuned in late had already panicked. They had turned off their radios and were praying or screaming or fleeing their homes.

By one estimate, about a million people believed Martians really had landed and were taking over the world. Mrs. Thomas from Trenton, New Jersey, was one. "We were petrified," she later said, describing her family's reaction. "We just looked at each other, scared out of our wits." Her neighbor had also heard the radio news and banged on Mrs. Thomas' door. "She had packed her seven kids in their car and she kept yelling, 'Come on! Let's get out of here!'"

Said Louis Winkler of New York City, "I heard the broadcast and almost had a heart attack."

In one block in Newark, twenty families rushed out of their homes with wet towels over their faces. They thought the towels would save them from the poison gas. Others hid in their cellars. Some packed their cars with food and drove off.

Thirteen-year-old Henry Sears lived near Grovers Mill. He, too, heard the news on the radio. Frightened, he took the radio downstairs to where his mother ran a tavern. He and his mother and about a dozen men listened to each new bulletin. At last the men jumped up and got their guns. They marched off to save Grovers Mill. They didn't find any Martians to shoot. But they did shoot up a wooden water tower. In the fog, they mistook it for a spaceship.

Within a few hours, most people learned the truth. There had been no explosions on Mars. Nothing had landed in a farmer's field. And there wasn't any Martian invasion. It was all made up.

People were furious at Orson Welles, the man who had directed the play. Welles had ended the show by saying, "[This was] the Mercury Theatre's own radio version of dressing up in a sheet and jumping out of a bush and saying 'Boo!'" Most people didn't see it that way. They had been really scared. Public anger was so great that Welles went into hiding. "He was gone for three or four days," recalled his boss, William Paley. "He was scared to death. It was a terrible thing for the American public to live through and he didn't want any part of it."

In time, the anger died down. People began to realize what a terrific show it had been. Welles had made it sound *so real*. Fifty years later, the people of Grovers Mill put up a statue to Welles. It showed him at the microphone with a family crowded around a radio. The statue was inscribed with these words: "One Million People Throughout the Country Believed That Martians Had Invaded the Earth."

If you have been timed while reading this article, enter your reading time below. Then turn to the Words-per-Minute Table on page 120 and look up your reading speed (words per minute). Enter your reading speed on the graph on page 121.

**Reading Time:** Selection 1

_____ : _____
MINUTES      SECONDS

**UNDERSTANDING IDEAS** Circle the letter of the best answer.

1. **The people who missed the beginning of the radio show**

   A  thought that World War II had been declared

   B  did not like the program

   C  thought that Martians had landed on Earth

   D  thought it was a joke

2. **Some men from Grovers Mill, New Jersey,**

   F  were prepared to defend their town

   G  charged a spaceship filled with Martians

   H  feared the rise of Adolph Hitler

   J  decided to leave the country

3. **The reason Orson Welles gave for broadcasting his radio play was that**

   A  there was no more music to play

   B  he wanted to warn people about Hitler

   C  he wanted to be remembered for something

   D  it was intended to be Halloween entertainment

4. **The fact that the people of Grovers Mill put up a statue of Welles shows that**

   F  he was never forgiven for his Halloween hoax

   G  he was forgiven for having caused such a panic

   H  they felt he was a war hero

   J  they felt he should be honored for performing a public service

5. **Which of the following statements is TRUE?**

   A  The events of this story took place in 1988.

   B  The public feared for their lives.

   C  The events described actually took place.

   D  Orson Welles was glad that people were terrified.

**SUMMARIZE** For each blank, choose the word that best completes the meaning of the paragraph.

| statue | directed | |
|--------|----------|------------|
| landed | angry | introduction |

On October 30, 1938, about a million people believed that Martians had _____ in Grovers Mill, New Jersey, and were taking over the world. They had missed the _____ to a play broadcast on the radio. Many people panicked. Later, when they learned the truth, they became _____ at Orson Welles, the man who had _____ the play. In time, the people of Grovers Mill forgave Welles and put up a _____ in his honor.

**IF YOU WERE THERE** What would you have done if you had heard the radio show that night? Write a brief paragraph explaining your actions. Be sure to include examples from the story to support your response.

_____

_____

_____

_____

_____

_____

# It's All in Your Mind

For Susan Davis, November 12, 1998, started like any other day. Davis was a high school cooking teacher at Warren County High School in McMinnville, Tennessee. As she got ready for her first class, she noticed a strange odor. It smelled like gasoline. Soon she felt dizzy. She became nauseated. Davis began to have trouble breathing and developed a splitting headache.

Before long, several students in her classes began to show the same symptoms. Principal George Bolding came to her room. He, too, noticed a strange odor. When he developed a headache, he sounded the fire alarm. Even after the school had been emptied, more students grew sick. Over one hundred students and staff were rushed to the emergency room of the hospital. Thirty-eight stayed in the hospital overnight.

The school remained closed for four days. Health and safety experts checked the school. So did fire and gas experts. They found nothing. So the school reopened. But the trouble hadn't gone away. Students quickly began to fall sick again.

Once again, ambulances rushed to the school. This time they took seventy-one people for treatment. No one could figure out what was happening. The victims did not come from just one room or one wing. Students and staff from all parts of the large high school fell ill.

Government officials closed the school. They checked for toxins. They tested the water and air. They drilled holes in the walls and wiped down surfaces. They flew a helicopter back and forth over the school looking for fumes. "They even had a cave expert check the underground water," said Bolding. "I didn't realize we had that many people in this country called air experts."

In all, twelve agencies, eight labs, and seven consulting firms were called in. They spent over three thousand hours looking for the cause. None of them found a thing. They found no medical cause. They found no environmental cause. There was only one explanation left. It was all in people's heads. The medical term is "mass psychogenic illness." It means that if people expect to get sick, they often do.

"[The illness is] much more common than most of us realize," said Dr. Timothy Jones. "The huge majority [of cases are not reported]. They tend to be dealt with locally and they go away and that's the end of it."

The school reopened again after two weeks. But Bolding and his staff remained on high alert for any odd smells. "I've smelled this place until I'm blue in the face," said Bolding. Still, he could not get rid of all odors—or all fears. "Any unusual smell and some people go bonkers," he said. After four months, some students detected a sweet smell. They soon fell ill. This time it turned out that the smell came from fish remains caught in a drain. The drains were cleaned out. And Bolding made sure no more fish were brought into the school.

Warren County isn't the only place where such incidents have occurred. In June of 1999, this same phenomenon cost Coca-Cola sixty million dollars. On June 8, a group of students in Belgium fell ill after drinking Coke products. Word spread. Over the next week more than two hundred people in Belgium and France became sick after drinking Coke and Fanta. They complained of nausea, vomiting, and dizziness.

Coca-Cola recalled millions of cans and bottles in Belgium and France. It was the biggest recall in the company's 114-year history. Some nations blocked the shipment of Coke products. On June 15, Belgium banned all Coke products.

It was a huge crisis for Coca-Cola. The company lost millions of dollars a day. The crisis was made worse by the media. Reporters passed on wild claims of illness. They also compared it to an earlier—and far more serious—scare over meat tainted with dioxin.

Coca-Cola officials tried their best to stop the tide of bad publicity. Chairman M. Douglas Ivester stated, "There's nothing wrong with Coke. I have tasted it myself. I've had the cans in my hands to assure myself. There is no health problem."

Ivester was proved right. Health officials tested Coke and found nothing harmful. They did find two small problems, however. In some cases, the carbon dioxide used to give Coke its fizz was slightly tainted. It was not enough to make a person sick, but it did give the drink a faint odor. In other cases, the cans themselves had picked up a foul odor. They had been carried on wooden pallets. At some point these pallets had been sprayed with a fungicide. Again, there was no health hazard. But fear combined with the odor produced mass psychogenic illness. Benoit Nemery, a toxicology expert, said, "I'm not saying [the victims] weren't ill. They were ill . . . but they were not poisoned." Added Nemery, "In vulgar terms, this is called mass hysteria."

After four weeks, the crisis passed. Coke products were put back on store shelves. Coke trucks in Belgium carried huge signs that read, "Your Coca-Cola Is Back." But like the people in Warren County, Coke officials had new respect for the power of the human imagination.

If you have been timed while reading this article, enter your reading time below. Then turn to the Words-per-Minute Table on page 120 and look up your reading speed (words per minute). Enter your reading speed on the graph on page 121.

**Reading Time:** Selection 2

_____ : _____
MINUTES      SECONDS

**UNDERSTANDING IDEAS** Circle the letter of the best answer.

**1. What seemed to be the cause of Sue Davis' symptoms?**

A something she had eaten

B a strange odor in her classroom

C her fear of getting ill

D her unruly students

**2. "Mass psychogenic illness" can be caused by**

F toxins

G the fear of getting sick

H poor air quality

J headaches

**3. In 1999, Coca-Cola products were found to be**

A harmless

B poisoned

C more popular in Europe than in the United States

D undrinkable

**4. Coca-Cola lost a great deal of money as a result of**

F bad management

G the economy

H a real health problem

J bad publicity

**SUMMARIZE** For each blank, choose the word that best completes the meaning of the paragraph.

| times | expect | experts | complained |
|---|---|---|---|
| group | harmful | power | |

If people _____ to get sick, they often do. In 1998, Warren County High School students and teachers fell ill, not once, but three _____. Air _____ found nothing. In 1999, a _____ of students in Belgium _____ of vomiting, nausea, and dizziness. Again, health officials found nothing _____. How can this be explained? The name for this is "mass psychogenic illness," and it shows the _____ of people's imaginations.

**IF YOU WERE THERE** Imagine that you were a teacher in Warren County High School. Write a brief paragraph explaining what you would tell health officials. Be sure to include examples from the story to support your response.

_____

_____

_____

_____

_____

_____

**USE CONTEXT CLUES** When you read, you may find a word whose meaning is unfamiliar to you. When that happens, you can look up the word's meaning in the dictionary. You can also find out what the word means by looking for context clues. These are words or sentences that come before or after the word. Context clues can be antonyms or synonyms of the unfamiliar word. They may also be an example or definition of the unfamiliar word.

Read each excerpt from the stories you just read. Circle the letter with the best meaning of the underlined word.

1. **The reporter tried to describe the creatures emerging from the spaceship. . . . "It's large as a bear and it glistens like wet leather. But that face. It. . . . it's indescribable."**
   A   incredible
   B   very ugly
   C   scary
   D   cannot be described

2. **But Bolding and his staff remained on high alert for any odd smells. . . . After four months, some students detected a sweet smell. They soon fell ill.**
   F   found, noticed
   G   ignored
   H   made, created
   J   invented

3. **Warren County isn't the only place where such incidents have occurred. In June of 1999, this same phenomenon cost Coca-Cola $60 million.**
   A   enemy
   B   illness, sickness
   C   situation, circumstance
   D   location

4. **Health officials tested Coke and found nothing harmful. . . . Again, there was no health hazard.**
   F   illness
   G   danger
   H   epidemic
   J   pollution

5. **"They were ill . . . but they were not poisoned. . . . In vulgar terms, this is called mass hysteria." After four weeks, the crisis passed.**
   A   an easily controlled reaction
   B   laughter
   C   a strong sense of denial
   D   extreme uncontrollable emotion

**PUT WORDS INTO CONTEXT** Complete the paragraph using the underlined words from the exercise on this page.

It's often hard to stop the spread of mass

_____. This kind of

_____ once cost the Coca-Cola

company millions of dollars. In 1999, the media had

reported a health _____ that had

begun in Belgium. Officials had _____

a faint odor that was on the outside of some cans. The

contents of the cans were safe. But the damage was

already done.

**SUFFIXES** A suffix is one or more letters added to the end of a word to change its meaning. For example, the suffix *–less* means "without." So, when you add the suffix *–less* to the end of the word *harm*, you get *harmless*, which means "without harm."

Use a dictionary to find the meaning of each suffix below. Match the suffix with its meaning on the right. Write the letter of the correct definition on the line. **One of the letters will be used twice.**

_____ **1.** -ly

_____ **2.** -ful

_____ **3.** -er

_____ **4.** -ness

_____ **5.** -able

_____ **6.** -ity

_____ **7.** -ment

**A** capable of, worthy of: *hugable*

**B** a person who: *preacher*

**C** state, condition, or quality: *brightness, normality*

**D** in the manner of, like: *strangely*

**E** result of an action or process: *advancement*

**F** characterized by, full of: *fearful*

**WRITE DEFINITIONS** On the line next to each word from the passages, write the new meaning of the word with the added suffix.

**1.** report + er = reporter

definition: _____

**2.** public + ity = publicity

definition: _____

**3.** treat + ment = treatment

definition: _____

**4.** quick + ly = quickly

definition: _____

**5.** harm + ful = harmful

definition: _____

**6.** manage + able = manageable

definition: _____

**7.** kind + ness = kindness

definition: _____

**FIND THE PURPOSE** Authors write to inform or teach, to persuade or convince, or to entertain. Sometimes there may be more than one purpose for writing. One example of multipurpose writing is the book review. The review informs the reader about the book, but it also persuades the reader to read or not read the book. Reviewers may also entertain their readers by making the review funny if the book lends itself to humor.

Read the chart below. Then answer the questions.

| AUTHOR'S PURPOSE | | |
|---|---|---|
| to inform (teach) | to persuade (convince) | to entertain (amuse) |
| • teach history, science, and other subjects | • argue for or against an issue in a review or editorial | • appeal to a reader's interest |
| • report an event | • convince people to buy | • make people laugh |
| • explain a process | • tell people how to act | • tell a personal story |
| • describe facts | • offer the best solution to a problem | • put words together in a poem |

1. If the CEO of Coca-Cola wrote an editorial for a newspaper in Belgium explaining there was nothing wrong with Coke, what would be the purpose?
   A  to inform
   B  to persuade
   C  to entertain
   D  all of the above

2. If "Trick or Treat" were an imaginary story, under which heading would it appear on the chart?
   F  to inform
   G  to persuade
   H  to entertain
   J  all of the above

3. A reviewer's recommendation about *War of the Worlds* by H. G. Wells should appear under which heading?
   A  to inform
   B  to persuade
   C  to entertain
   D  all of the above

4. An author writes a serious essay stating an opinion that alien encounters are bound to occur. What two purposes does the author have?
   F  to entertain and to persuade
   G  to inform and to entertain
   H  to inform and to persuade
   J  all of the above

**WRITE WITH A PURPOSE** Write a topic sentence for each of the purposes you have learned.

to inform: _____

to persuade: _____

to entertain: _____

**VERIFYING EVIDENCE** As a reader, it's up to you to weigh the evidence being offered in any piece of writing. When the author has written to inform or persuade, you must verify or confirm the evidence being offered and judge just how believable that evidence is. Pretend you came across the following item in your daily newspaper. Read the article and then choose the best answer for each question.

[1] Mabel Mercer reported today that a spaceship the size of a SUV landed in her backyard. [2] Mercer reported that the aliens came to her back door and introduced themselves as Martians. [3] She said the aliens were mild-mannered. [4] Mercer's husband, Joe, was home at the time of the incident. [5] "I saw these short, squat, two-headed creatures. [6] They gave me the fright of my life." [7] Experts say that each year thousands of Americans report visits from aliens. [8] Some people have even tried entering their spacecrafts. [9] Dr. Lenore Simmons of the State Department said, "People who claim to have been visited by aliens are just trying to get attention."

1. **Which is the best source for verifying what experts have said?**

   A  a supermarket tabloid

   B  the encyclopedia

   C  your community newsletter

   D  a monthly magazine article entitled *"Is There Life on Mars?"*

2. **Which of the following sentences offers the most convincing evidence that Mabel Mercer might be telling the truth?**

   F  Sentences 1 and 2

   G  Sentence 2

   H  Sentences 3–7

   J  Sentence 9

**JUDGE THE EVIDENCE** To persuade the reader of an opinion or story, the author often provides evidence. It is up to the reader to judge if the evidence presented is believable or not.

1. **Which statement best supports the opinion that aliens have had contact with humans?**

   A  There may be life on Mars after all.

   B  Each year, thousands of people say that they've met aliens.

   C  Some people appear to have vivid imaginations.

   D  People have seen movies about alien encounters.

2. **Which statement best supports the fact that the Orson Welles radio play was just a hoax?**

   F  People fled their homes.

   G  The men of Grovers Mill were prepared to shoot the Martians, but they couldn't find any Martians to shoot.

   H  Bombs were being dropped on New Jersey.

   J  Families put towels over their faces to protect themselves from poison gas.

**PERSUADE WITH EVIDENCE** Write two sentences persuading your reader about a strange thing that has happened to you. The first sentence should summarize your story. The second sentence should try to prove that your story is true.

_____

_____

_____

_____

_____

_____

## "In Deep, Deep Trouble"

Donald Mell, an Associated Press photographer, thought it was odd. Earlier, he had noticed a green Mercedes parked outside the tennis club. Curtains were drawn over the rear windows. Now Mell saw the car again. This time it was parked near his apartment in Beirut, Lebanon. "That's weird," he thought.

But Mell didn't think much more of it. It was about 8:00 A.M. on March 16, 1985. He had just finished a tennis match with Terry Anderson, the chief AP correspondent in the Middle East. Anderson was dropping off Mell at his apartment. Mell never mentioned the Mercedes to Anderson. After all, Beirut in 1985 was a war-torn city. There were lots of strange and menacing sights in the city.

Then, without warning, the doors of the Mercedes flew open. Three armed men hopped out. Before Anderson or Mell could react, one of the men yanked open the driver's-side door of Anderson's car. He pressed his pistol to Anderson's head. "Get out!" shouted the man. "I will shoot. I will shoot."

"Okay," said Anderson.

The man pulled off Anderson's glasses and forced him out of the car. "Come, come quickly," he demanded.

Anderson glanced at Mell, who was standing on the other side of Anderson's car. He wanted the photographer to run away. But Mell stood frozen, unable to move. There was really nothing he could do to help Anderson. After all, the men had guns. Mell was armed with nothing more than a tennis racket. The men forced Anderson into the back of the Mercedes and sped off, leaving Mell behind. It was Anderson they wanted.

The kidnappers pushed Anderson onto the floor between the front and rear seats. They tossed a coarse blanket over him. One kidnapper rested his feet on Anderson while holding a gun to his neck. The car sped through the streets of Beirut. One of the men said to Anderson in a calm voice, "Don't worry. It's political."

At first, Anderson's heart was beating so fast he didn't know what to think. As he wrote in his 1993 memoir, *Kidnapped*, "There wasn't any real fear yet—it was drowned by adrenaline. Just a loud, repeating mental refrain: 'Anderson, you stupid [fool], you're in deep, deep trouble.'"

Anderson's kidnapping *was* political. The three men belonged to Islamic Jihad. This group had already kidnapped other Westerners. The Islamic Jihad hated Westerners. They especially hated Americans. Kidnapping was part of their plan to attack Americans and American interests in the Middle East.

After about twenty minutes, the car pulled into a garage. Anderson could hear the garage door closing. The kidnappers removed the blanket and put a dirty cloth over Anderson's face. They wrapped the cloth in tape. Then they pulled off his tennis shoes.

The kidnappers had told Anderson not to worry. But in truth he had plenty to worry about. When he told the men that he was a journalist, they accused him of being a spy. Then they pressed him for information about other Americans in Beirut. Anderson said he couldn't tell them anything.

"We can make you," said one of the men.

"I know you can try," said Anderson. "You can hurt me. But I can't give you the names of my friends."

"We have electricity. You know?"

"Yes, I know. But I still won't give you names."

Despite torture, Anderson refused to talk. The beatings were bad. But for him the worst part was the uncertainty. He had no idea how long the kidnappers would keep him. Anderson had to live day to day and hope for the best. He passed his time in a dank cell, often blindfolded and chained.

His captivity almost destroyed him. Every day Anderson had to deal with fear, grief, and a sense of hopelessness. He was later asked how he survived.

"You just do what you have to do," he answered. "You wake up every day and you summon up the energy from somewhere, even when you think you haven't got it, and you get through the day. And you do it day after day after day."

The days turned into weeks. The weeks turned into months and then years. The Islamic Jihad released other hostages, but not Anderson. In 1987, his kidnappers refused to let him send home a Christmas message. That was too much for Anderson. In despair, he beat his head against a wall until it bled.

The kidnappers held Terry Anderson for a little over six years. Finally, though, a new leader took over in Iran, the nation that supported Islamic Jihad. The new leader wanted to ease tensions with the West. He pushed the kidnappers to release Anderson. On December 4, 1991, they did. After 2,455 days, Terry Anderson became a free man once more.

If you have been timed while reading this article, enter your reading time below. Then turn to the Words-per-Minute Table on page 120 and look up your reading speed (words per minute). Enter your reading speed on the graph on page 121.

**Reading Time:** Selection 1

_____ : _____
MINUTES    SECONDS

**UNDERSTANDING IDEAS** Circle the letter of the best answer.

**1. Which statement belongs in the empty box?**

A Anderson writes a book about his experience.

B Donald Mell joins Anderson.

C Anderson becomes a spy.

D Anderson is held captive for almost six years.

**2. Anderson was kidnapped by the members of Islamic Jihad because**

F he was a journalist

G he had written a book about them

H they wanted to oppose the West and Americans

J they wanted to come to the United States

**3. Why was Anderson released after six years?**

A He had served his full sentence.

B Iran's new leader wanted a better relationship with the West.

C He was no longer of any use to the kidnappers.

D He had behaved well enough.

**4. The fact that Anderson was not "broken" by his ordeal shows that**

F he had a lot of energy

G he had been tortured

H his sense of hope was stronger than his sense of despair

J he had never been terribly worried

**SUMMARIZE** For each blank, choose the word that best completes the meaning of the paragraph.

| released | kidnapped | |
|---|---|---|
| | | leader |
| chained | spy | |

When members of Islamic Jihad

_____ Terry Anderson in 1985, he

found himself in deep trouble. Because he was a

journalist, they accused him of being a

_____. They tortured him and kept

him _____ and blindfolded

in a cell for nearly six years. When a new

_____ took over in Iran, the

kidnappers _____ Anderson.

**IF YOU WERE THERE** Imagine that you were kidnapped. Write a brief paragraph explaining how you would keep yourself alive and hopeful. Be sure to include examples from the story to support your response.

_____

_____

_____

_____

_____

_____

_____

# Prisoner in Afghanistan

On August 3, 2001, American Dayna Curry walked out of a friend's house in Afghanistan. The foreign aid worker didn't get far. She was quickly arrested. Her crime? She was charged with spreading Christianity. Under the harsh laws of Afghanistan's Taliban rulers, she could be put to death if she was found guilty.

Curry wasn't the only one arrested. Her friend, Heather Mercer, came out of the house moments later. The Taliban promptly arrested her, too. They also arrested four other women and two men. All were foreign aid workers from an agency called Shelter Now International.

Curry later described the panic she felt when she was detained. "I was in a car on my own for two hours," she recalled. "That's when I felt more fear than I ever had. You actually feel fire going through your body."

The Taliban put Curry and the five other women in a cell. The two men were housed in a separate cell. The Taliban had a reputation for cruelty, especially toward women. But they treated these foreign women with care. "I couldn't believe it when one of the jailers told me, 'I love you as my sister and I'm not going to let anything happen to you,'" said Curry. Why were the Taliban jailers so nice? "They tell you that, as foreigners, you are their guests, and they treat you really well," explained Curry.

Most of the time she and the others could send mail. They were allowed to sing and pray. The women even got a few meals cooked by the commander's personal cook. Still, the experience was no picnic. The prisoners were often moved from prison to prison in Kabul, the Afghan capital. These prisons were filthy. There were flies all over the place. One toilet served 40 prisoners. The food came with ants. The water used for baths was frigid.

The foreign women were questioned but never beaten. "It would disgrace them to touch us," said Mercer.

Those rules, however, did not apply to Afghan women. One day Mercer had tea with two Afghan women prisoners. The female warden had said it was okay. Apparently, it wasn't. Some unknown rule had been broken. When Mercer left the room after the tea, the warden grabbed a piece of rubber hose and beat the two Afghans. When Mercer heard their cries, she said, "If I've done something wrong it's my fault. Hit me." But the warden just continued to beat the Afghans.

Such beatings happened all the time. "We saw some pretty atrocious things happening to the [Afghan] prisoners," said Mercer. "Women were being beaten until they bled." Most of these women had done nothing wrong by Western standards. They had been arrested for running away from husbands who beat them!

September 11, 2001, brought change to Afghanistan. That was the day terrorists flew planes into the World Trade Center and the Pentagon. The man held responsible for the terrorist attacks was Osama bin Laden. He was from Saudi Arabia. But he was living in Afghanistan with the Taliban. This made the Taliban the enemy of the United States.

The September 11 attacks really frightened Curry and the other prisoners. They figured the Americans would begin bombing Afghanistan. And they were right. The bombing started on October 7. Some of the bombs came dangerously close. "Our prison was shaking," said Mercer. "All we could do was sit and pray."

On the night of November 12, the eight prisoners were asleep. Suddenly the doors to their cells burst open. Taliban soldiers ordered them to pack up. They were told they had to move fast. The prisoners were herded into a van and driven toward the town of Kandahar. The van was full of rocket launchers and men with guns. "It was probably the first time I really, really felt we were in danger," said Curry.

The prisoners spent one night freezing in a metal shipping container. The next day they moved again. This time they went to the southern town of Ghazni. On the morning of November 14, American planes bombed the town. The prisoners heard the bombs falling and rocket launchers being fired. When they looked out the window, they saw the Taliban soldiers running. "At the time we didn't know they were fleeing," said Mercer.

There was nothing the prisoners could do. So they ate breakfast. Suddenly all the noise outside stopped. It grew very peaceful. For several minutes there was nothing but silence. But that didn't last. "All of a sudden we heard, at the front door, men coming back and banging down the prison door," said Mercer. "We thought it was the Taliban soldiers coming back and that this was the end of the road."

It wasn't the Taliban. It was an Afghan who opposed the Taliban. He was part of a group called the Northern Alliance. This group was fighting to overthrow the Taliban. The man walked to their cell and shouted, "You're free! You're free! The city is free, the Taliban have left." The happy prisoners ran into the street to join the celebration. The next day, Curry and her friends were on a helicopter to freedom. Their nightmare in Afghanistan was over.

If you have been timed while reading this article, enter your reading time below. Then turn to the Words-per-Minute Table on page 120 and look up your reading speed (words per minute). Enter your reading speed on the graph on page 121.

**Reading Time:** Selection 2

_____ : _____
MINUTES    SECONDS

**UNDERSTANDING IDEAS** Circle the letter of the best answer.

1. **Why were Curry and Mercer arrested in Afghanistan?**
   A They were charged with being members of a foreign aid organization.
   B They were charged with spreading Christianity.
   C They had not gotten proper visas.
   D The Taliban had not invited them into their country.

2. **During the period they were held captive, the women**
   F were mistreated by their captors
   G witnessed Taliban cruelty toward Afghan women
   H felt comfortable and safe
   J learned to accept the Taliban's views

3. **What did NOT happen as a result of the September 11 terrorist attack on the World Trade Center and the Pentagon?**
   A The women's prison was set on fire.
   B The United States began bombing Afghanistan.
   C The women were afraid of getting killed.
   D The Northern Alliance set the prisoners free.

4. **The women were released from prison by**
   F a member of an Afghan group that opposed the Taliban
   G a member of the U.S. military
   H their Taliban guards
   J Osama bin Laden

**SUMMARIZE** For each blank, choose the word that best completes the meaning of the paragraph.

| harmed | workers | |
|---|---|---|
| prisons | arrested | released |

One day, without warning, the Taliban arrested Dayna Curry, Heather Mercer, and several other foreign aid _____. The women were _____ for "spreading Christianity." Though they were kept in filthy _____ and moved from place to place, their captors never _____ them. Eventually, the women were _____ when the Northern Alliance chased the Taliban out of Ghazni.

**IF YOU WERE THERE** Write a brief paragraph explaining what you would do if taken prisoner by an enemy country. Be sure to include examples from the story to support your response.

_____
_____
_____
_____
_____

67

**USE CONTEXT CLUES** When you read, you may find a word whose meaning is unfamiliar to you. When that happens, you can look up the word's meaning in the dictionary. You can also find out what the word means by looking for context clues. These are words or sentences that come before or after the word. Context clues can be antonyms or synonyms of the unfamiliar word. They may also be an example or definition of the unfamiliar word.

Read each excerpt from the stories you just read. Circle the letter with the best meaning of the underlined word.

1. **Curry later described the panic she felt when she was underlined detained. "I was in a car on my own for two hours," she recalled.**
   A  held as prisoner
   B  feeling afraid
   C  remembered
   D  accused

2. **"We saw some pretty atrocious things happening to the [Afghan] prisoners," said Mercer. "Women were being beaten until they bled."**
   F  awful, horrible
   G  extremely quiet
   H  wasteful
   J  quite sorrowful

3. **But for [Anderson] the worst part was the uncertainty. He had no idea how long the kidnappers would keep him.**
   A  helplessness
   B  cruelty
   C  not knowing
   D  trying to find out

4. **But Mell stood frozen, unable to move. There was really nothing he could do to help Anderson.**
   F  motionless
   G  solidly
   H  polarized
   J  unhappily

5. **"You wake up every day and you summon up the energy from somewhere, even when you think you haven't got it, you get through the day."**
   A  remove
   B  display
   C  increase
   D  call up

**PUT WORDS INTO CONTEXT** Complete the paragraph using the underlined words from the exercise on this page.

During the time they were being

_____ in an Afghan prison,

Curry and Mercer were not mistreated. Terry Anderson,

however, was not spared from

_____ conditions. He was

tortured and kept chained and blindfolded in a dark,

damp cell. The beatings were bad, but the

_____ was the worst part.

How he was able to _____ up

the courage to get through each day for almost six

years is a miracle.

**USING EXACT WORDS** You can make your writing come alive for the reader by using exact, or highly specific, words. Exact words help to create vivid mental pictures in the mind of your reader. For example, which sentence gives you a better image? (1) Terry Anderson spent six years in a prison cell. (2) Terry Anderson passed his time in a dank cell, often blindfolded and chained. Sentence 2 gives you a specific mental picture because of the use of vivid adjectives. In sentence 1, you aren't sure of the kind of conditions to picture.

Read these sentences from the stories. Choose the MOST exact adjective or verb to replace the underlined word.

1. **There were lots of strange and menacing sights in the city.**

   A  surprising

   B  common

   C  bizarre

   D  funny

2. **The man pulled off Anderson's glasses and forced him out of the car.**

   F  obtained

   G  stopped

   H  received

   J  yanked off

3. **In despair, he beat his head against a wall until it bled.**

   A  slapped

   B  banged

   C  drove

   D  throbbed

4. **The Islamic Jihad released other hostages, but not Anderson.**

   F  moved

   G  freed

   H  apologized

   J  challenged

5. **The happy prisoners ran into the street to join the celebration.**

   A  overjoyed

   B  positive

   C  calm

   D  peaceful

**ANALOGIES** As you have seen in previous exercises, analogies show relationships and patterns between words. The relationships can be very different things, not just synonyms and antonyms. For example, *hat* is to *head* as *glove* is to *hand*. The first words (*hat* and *glove*) are meant to cover the second words (*head* and *hand*). For each blank, choose an underlined word from the exercise on this page to correctly complete the analogy. In most cases, you will only use one of the underlined words.

1. *Near* is to *close* as

   _____ is to *yanked*.

2. *Quick* is to *fast* as

   _____ is to *bizarre*.

3. *Tall* is to *short* as

   _____ is to *sad*.

4. *Kept* is to *possessed* as

   _____ is to *let go*.

5. *Shoved* is to *pushed* as

   _____ is to *hit*.

# SUMMARIZING

**PRACTICE SUMMARIZING** As you now know, a summary retells the main points of a story. Summaries do not attempt to recount every detail. The reason summaries are useful is that they are always shorter than the original piece. For example, if you look up a TV guide in the newspaper, there is often a summary of what the show is about. A sentence is usually enough to summarize a half-hour program.

Practice writing one-sentence summaries of these news articles. Use only one sentence. You decide what the article will be about based on the headline. The first one is done for you.

**News Article and One-sentence Summary**

1. "Heroes of 9/11"

   _Reporter Sara Frost interviews rescue workers who were at the scene of the World Trade Center on September 11._

2. "Three Hostages Taken at Gunpoint"

3. "Mayor Wins Second Term"

4. "U.S. Troops Search for Osama bin Laden"

**SUMMARIZE THE STORIES** In the space provided, write a one-paragraph summary of each of the selections. Be sure to include only the main points from each selection.

### "In Deep, Deep Trouble"

### "Prisoner in Afghanistan"

**MAKE PREDICTIONS** You can make predictions, or educated guesses, based on what you already know. For example, you already know that the United States has responded to terrorist attacks by bombing countries that protect leaders of terrorist organizations. Based on this knowledge, you can reasonably predict that if there is another terrorist attack, the U.S. will do the same thing again. Read this passage, and answer the following questions based on what you know after reading the story.

[1] Intelligence agents are actively looking for terrorists around the world. [2] The hunt for terrorists and their leaders has proved to be very frustrating. [3] Rough terrain and language barriers are just a few of the difficult hurdles that the searches must overcome. [4] Still, what drives the manhunt is the assumption that known terrorists' leaders are still alive. [5] Until there's reason to believe otherwise, the hunt will go on.

1. **Which sentence in the passage helps you predict that the search for terrorists' leaders may stop at some point?**

   **A** Sentence 1

   **B** Sentence 2

   **C** Sentence 3

   **D** Sentence 5

2. **Suppose U.S. intelligence says that a known terrorist leader may be crossing the rugged mountain ranges on horseback. What might the special troops do next?**

   **F** call off the search

   **G** blanket the mountains with terrorists

   **H** begin searching the mountains

   **J** hope the terrorist gets lost in the mountains

3. **What would a skeptic most likely say about the search for a known terrorist?**

   **A** It's worth all the trouble.

   **B** It will help advance the cause of peace.

   **C** It's impossible to find terrorists.

   **D** It will earn world respect.

**JUDGE THE BASIS OF A PREDICTION** For predictions to be reasonably accurate, they must be based on what you know to be factual information. Choose the best answer.

1. **Which statement helps you predict what a skeptic's position would be?**

   **A** Skeptics, by nature, are doubtful and critical.

   **B** Most skeptics believe that terrorists are brave.

   **C** A few skeptics are optimistic and positive in attitude.

   **D** Most skeptics support the search for terrorists.

2. **Which statement helps you predict that another terrorist attack could take place somewhere in the world?**

   **F** The United States is actively searching for terrorists.

   **G** Terrorists no longer feel that acts of terror benefit their cause.

   **H** There are organizations dedicated to terrorist purposes.

   **J** A closer look at terrorist organizations shows that they are dying out.

**PREDICT WHAT YOU WOULD DO** Write a brief paragraph explaining what you would do if you were searching for known leaders of terrorist organizations. Use examples from the stories you just read to explain your predictions.

_____

_____

_____

_____

_____

_____

# UNIT 7
# TRAGIC GAMES

## SELECTION 1
# Bonfire Disaster

72

"The bonfire started as a symbol of our burning desire to support our football team," said Will Hurd, the student president. "It has now turned into an act of kinship, an act of love."

Hurd made this comment in 1999. He was speaking about a bonfire tradition that dated back to 1909. That's when students at Texas A&M (Agricultural and Mechanical College of Texas) gathered a pile of trash and scrap wood. Then they lit it. Each year after that the students, nicknamed Aggies, built another bonfire. They kept building the pile higher and higher until, in the late 1960s, it reached nearly 110 feet. That was too high and too dangerous. University officials told the students to cut the height of future bonfires in half. So students contented themselves with 55-foot bonfires. They built one every year before the football game with their arch rival, the University of Texas.

In 1999, it was no different. Building such a big bonfire took weeks of hard work. First, the students cut down enough trees to make about 7,000 logs. Each log was the size of a telephone pole. Then they dug a 15-foot hole to bury the center pole. They made this pole by gluing two poles end to end. The students strengthened the center pole with fasteners and steel cables.

They placed four supporting poles about 150 feet from the center. After that, the students brought in cranes to layer the huge logs one on top of the other in the shape of a pyramid. The logs were wired together. When it was finished, the bonfire weighed more than 2 million pounds.

Students worked on the bonfire around the clock. That was part of the tradition. The students called it "push time." The bonfire was mostly a student project. The leaders were eighteen juniors and seniors known as "Red Pots." The name came from the red helmets they wore. Hundreds of other students helped to build the bonfire.

Freshman Paul Jones was eager to help. On November 17, he and some friends volunteered to work the midnight to 6:00 A.M. shift. Jones later said, "This was push time for the bonfire. I was excited. We went out [to the bonfire] in a caravan, fifteen of us. We were laughing and joking in the car. Being in a group is important here—it's all part of the family feeling."

The good times came to an end on November 18, at 2:28 A.M. At that point there were about seventy students putting the finishing touches on the bonfire. Twenty-year-old Tommy Balez was taking a break. He was standing about 150 feet from the bonfire when he heard a crash. He couldn't believe it. The entire bonfire was collapsing! "There was a loud crack, then another loud crash when it went over," said Balez.

"It just toppled over," said Diana Estrada, who was standing about 200 yards away. "We ran over there as fast as we could. We could see legs sticking out and hear people screaming."

Shaun Humphrey had walked away from the bonfire to get a drink of water. Suddenly, he heard "this loud pop—like a gunshot." Humphrey ran to the pile to see if he could help anyone. "All you could hear was screaming and crying. It was probably the most horrific thing I'll ever hear. That'll haunt me forever."

Brandon Jozwiak was working on the bonfire when it collapsed. "The logs crumbled like dominoes beneath me," he later said. "I thought, 'What am I going to do?' But there was nothing I could do except ride the wave. It was like being in an avalanche of logs."

Jozwiak was trapped between two logs about ten feet above the ground. Each time he took a deep breath, the logs just crushed him more. He whispered to himself, "Maybe this is it." Then he felt a log give way. Jozwiak was able to squirm free.

Jozwiak was lucky. The bonfire was built so it would collapse in on itself as it burned. But something had gone wrong and the bonfire had now collapsed to one side. Students caught on that side were crushed or trapped under the weight of hundreds of logs. More than a hundred rescue workers rushed to the

scene. Along with students, they worked all day carefully picking through the fallen logs. Tommy Belez spent more than twelve hours with a rescue crew. "I'm staying until I know everybody is out," he said.

Sadly, some people did not make it out. Twelve students died. Twenty-seven others were injured, some seriously. Shaun Humphrey held the hand of one student buried under the logs, urging him to hang on. Finally an emergency worker tapped Humphrey on the shoulder and told him it was no use. The student was dead.

Dr. Ray Bowen, the university president, called the accident "a great tragedy." He also canceled future bonfires. Meanwhile, Texas A&M graduates came together to mourn the event. Lieutenant Governor Rick Perry graduated from Texas A&M in 1972. On the night of the collapse, he told a group of mourners, "We will remember [the dead] as long as there is a Texas A&M and Aggie spirit, and that, my friends, is forever."

If you have been timed while reading this article, enter your reading time below. Then turn to the Words-per-Minute Table on page 120 and look up your reading speed (words per minute). Enter your reading speed on the graph on page 121.

**Reading Time:** Selection 1

_____ : _____
MINUTES        SECONDS

**UNDERSTANDING IDEAS** Circle the letter of the best answer.

**1. Which of the following statements is NOT true?**

**A** The bonfire was an old tradition.

**B** The bonfire showed support for the school's football team.

**C** Students cut the height of bonfires in half after the tragedy.

**D** The accident killed and injured some of the students.

**2. Based on the story, what does *push time* mean?**

**F** the amount of effort it takes to build a bonfire

**G** the last practice of the football team before the big game

**H** the time it takes to layer the huge logs

**J** the round-the-clock work shifts that finish building the bonfire

**3. Brandon Jozwiak survived the collapse of the bonfire because**

**A** he wasn't pinned by any of the logs

**B** he had just completed his shift

**C** a log gave way and released him

**D** he was standing off to the side

**4. As a result of the 1999 bonfire tragedy, the university president**

**F** was replaced by the Lieutenant Governor

**G** ended the bonfire tradition

**H** expelled the student leaders who were in charge

**J** closed the school

**SUMMARIZE** For each blank, choose the word that best completes the meaning of the paragraph.

| side | pole | collapsed |
| tragedy | chance | trapped |

In 1999, an act of team spirit became a great _____ when a bonfire at Texas A&M _____. More than 7,000 logs, each the size of a telephone _____, were used. This year, for some reason, before anyone had a _____ to light the fire, the 7,000 logs started falling to one _____. Students found themselves crushed or _____ under the weight.

**IF YOU WERE THERE** Write a brief paragraph suggesting a tradition that would show school spirit. Be sure to include examples from the story to support your response.

_____
_____
_____
_____
_____
_____
_____

# Soccer Riot

Ellis Park in Johannesburg, South Africa, held 60,000 people. But it wasn't nearly big enough to hold all the people who wanted to see the game. The soccer match between the Orlando Pirates and the Kaizer Chiefs was the biggest of the season. They were the two best teams in South Africa.

South African fans usually bought their tickets at the stadium on the day of the game. But for this game Kaizer Motaung, the owner of the Chiefs, sold 15,000 tickets in advance. The other remaining 45,000 were sold on the night of the match. They were general admission tickets. That meant there were no assigned seat numbers. Rob Moore, another soccer team owner, said, "Not assigning . . . seat numbers for a game like this is a recipe for disaster."

More than 75,000 fans showed up to see the match on the evening of April 11, 2001. So there were 60,000 people in the stadium and another 15,000 wanting to get in. That was bad enough. But to make things worse, some vendors sold counterfeit tickets. Other fans bribed ticket takers to let them into the stadium without tickets. At least two thousand extra fans squeezed into Ellis Park. "The stadium was full," said Louis Shipalan, a security guard on duty. "There was no place to stand."

That still left many thousands outside. Some even had tickets. In any case, many of these fans had come from far away. They didn't want to be shut out now. But how could they get in?

Solomzi Matu was on duty as a security guard. He described what happened next. "The pressure started about ten minutes before the 8:00 P.M. kickoff, when people outside the perimeter area realized they would not get in," he said. "Some of them had tickets. Yet we were instructed not to let anyone in because the stadium was full."

Soon angry fans were pressing against the metal fence that kept them out. The Chiefs scored first to take a 1 – 0 lead. A few minutes later, the Pirates scored, tying the game. "The pressure just soared," said Matu. "There were so many people, thousands of them. We are not armed and could not handle the crush."

Steven Taljaard, the manager of Ellis Park, said later, "We just could not contain the crowd. They started physically removing the fence. The more we said it was sold out, the more aggressive they became."

At last, the frustrated fans toppled the metal fence. As it fell, it trapped several people. The fans on the outside then ran into the stadium. They rushed over the fallen fence, crushing to death those trapped under it. Within seconds, the initial rush turned into a full-fledged stampede. According to witnesses, police responded by firing tear gas into the crowd. That just led to more panic. Everyone was pushing, shoving, and screaming.

"I was pushed from behind," said Pirates fan Ernest Sibane. "The next thing I knew I was down, and somebody who was next to me bit my hand. I later learned that that person died."

For a while, the referees were unaware of what was happening in the stands. So the soccer game proceeded as usual. By the time officials stopped the match, twenty people were dead. Some died of suffocation. Others were trampled.

But stopping the game didn't end the madness. Some people apparently did not realize that fans were dying. They shouted for the match to continue. The public address announcer tried to calm the crowd, speaking the local Xhosa language. But by then the mob was out of control. The stampeding continued.

Ambulances raced to Ellis Park. But they were blocked by traffic and the scaffolding set up for TV cameras. Helicopters had to fly in to remove the dead and injured. By the time they finished, the death toll stood at 43. Another 158 people were injured.

Many of the dead and injured were children. One fourteen-year-old girl was killed during the stampede. After the crazed fans ran by, a security guard tried to pull her free. It was too late.

Oupa Mabaso, an executive with the Pirates, said, "It is a hurting thing. It put a black mark on South African soccer."

Ellis Park was the worst soccer disaster in South African history. But it was the worst by only one death. In 1991, the same two teams played in the small mining town of Orkney. A similar stampede broke out, killing 42. Clearly, organizers of the sport hadn't learned from the Ellis Park incident. South Africans could only hope that they would learn from this one.

If you have been timed while reading this article, enter your reading time below. Then turn to the Words-per-Minute Table on page 120 and look up your reading speed (words per minute). Enter your reading speed on the graph on page 121.

**Reading Time:** Selection 2

_____ : _____
MINUTES    SECONDS

**UNDERSTANDING IDEAS** Circle the letter of the best answer.

1. **Which factor was NOT a contributing cause of the soccer stampede?**

   **A** There were no assigned seats.

   **B** A loud thunderstorm began.

   **C** More fans showed up than there was room for.

   **D** Fans with tickets could not get into the stadium.

2. **The soccer game between the Pirates and the Chiefs**

   **F** ended in tragedy

   **G** had to be stopped

   **H** was the biggest of the season

   **J** all of the above

3. **Based on the evidence in this story, readers can conclude that**

   **A** the owner of the Chiefs was responsible for the tragedy

   **B** having assigned seats is not important

   **C** an angry mob is hard to control

   **D** players should have kept playing

4. **One reason that officials could not calm the crowd was that**

   **F** the public address system was not working

   **G** by the time they tried, it was too late to stop the riot

   **H** too many children had been hurt

   **J** the players refused to start the game

**SUMMARIZE** For each blank, choose the word that best completes the meaning of the paragraph.

| death | stampede | |
|---|---|---|
| sporting | people | happened |

When soccer fans rioted in South Africa, many _____ died. Fans rioted on April 11, 2001, in Johannesburg and the _____ toll reached 43. In 1991, a _____ of people killed 42 fans. Something similar had _____ at the match ten years earlier. It seems that organizers of _____ events hadn't learned anything.

**IF YOU WERE THERE** Write a brief paragraph explaining what you might do to keep fans safe if you were organizing a sporting event. Be sure to include examples from the story to support your response.

_____
_____
_____
_____
_____
_____
_____
_____

**USE CONTEXT CLUES** When you read, you may find a word whose meaning is unfamiliar to you. When that happens, you can look up the word's meaning in the dictionary. You can also find out what the word means by looking for context clues. These are words or sentences that come before or after the word. Context clues can be antonyms or synonyms of the unfamiliar word. They may also be an example or definition of the unfamiliar word.

Read each excerpt from the stories you just read. Circle the letter with the best meaning of the underlined word.

1. "[The] bonfire started as a symbol of our burning desire to support our football team. . . . It has now turned into an act of kinship, an act of love."

   A worship

   B impulse

   C sense of family, close connection

   D anger, frustration

2. "We went out [to the bonfire] in a caravan, fifteen of us. . . . Being in a group is important here—it's all part of the family feeling."

   F a spirit of excitement

   G a group of people who travel together

   H at a moment's notice

   J rented bus

3. The entire bonfire was collapsing! "There was a loud crack, then another loud crash when it went over," said Balez.

   A finishing

   B making noise

   C on fire

   D falling down

4. "They started physically removing the fence. The more we said it was sold out, the more aggressive they became."

   F wanting to attack, violent

   G friendly

   H calm and giving

   J unusual

5. They rushed over the fallen fence, crushing to death those trapped under it. Within seconds, the initial rush turned into a full-fledged stampede.

   A death

   B trap

   C crowd moving in panic

   D flowing river

**PUT WORDS INTO CONTEXT** Complete the paragraph using the underlined words from the exercise on this page.

The soccer riot in South Africa was caused by anger, greed, and poor planning. Desperate fans became _____ when they could not get into the stadium. They removed a fence and rushed in, causing a _____. In contrast, the tragedy in Texas was caused by a freak accident. Texans will always feel a strong _____ with students who died that day. Even members of the rival football team mourned the loss of lives.

**MULTIPLE MEANINGS** Many words are spelled alike but have different meanings. You can determine the meaning of a word by seeing how it is used in a sentence.

Read the definitions of each word. On the line, write the meaning of the underlined word as it is used in the sentence.

> **match:** 1. a person or thing that is equal to or like another 2. a game or contest

1. The soccer <u>match</u> between the Orlando Pirates and the Kaizer Chiefs was the biggest of the season.

   _____

2. Greg is a good tennis player, but he's no <u>match</u> for Beth.

   _____

> **game:** 1. a sport or contest with certain rules 2. full of spirit or courage

3. A few minutes later the Pirates scored, tying the <u>game</u>.

   _____

4. Are you <u>game</u> for a swim in the lake?

   _____

> **guard:** 1. a person who keeps watch and protects 2. a player in a football or basketball game

5. Solomzi Matu was on duty as a security <u>guard</u>.

   _____

6. Joe played the position of <u>guard</u> for the high school football team last year.

   _____

> **log:** 1. a long piece of a tree cut with the bark still on 2. the travel record of a ship or plane flight

7. Each <u>log</u> was the size of a telephone pole.

   _____

8. The ship's captain kept a <u>log</u>.

   _____

> **crane:** 1. a large bird with thin legs and a long neck 2. a large machine used to lift and move heavy objects 3. to stretch out the neck in order to see better

9. After that, the students brought in <u>cranes</u> to layer the huge logs one on top of the other in the shape of a pyramid.

   _____

10. The people in the back had to <u>crane</u> their necks to see the parade.

   _____

**ORGANIZE THE FACTS** The two stories you read in this unit are alike in some ways and different in other ways. A Venn diagram can show how they are alike and different. Look at the Venn diagram below. Then choose the best answer to each question.

"BONFIRE DISASTER"
College sport

BOTH
Sports disaster

"SOCCER RIOT"
Professional game

1. **Which of the following details belongs in the oval marked BOTH?**

   **A**  occurred in the United States

   **B**  innocent sports fans died

   **C**  Brandon Jozniak was trapped between two logs.

   **D**  could never happen again

2. **Which detail does NOT belong in the oval marked "Bonfire Disaster"?**

   **F**  Sports fans showed support for their team.

   **G**  The bonfire has been a tradition since 1909.

   **H**  Someone purposefully caused the bonfire to fall.

   **J**  Students worked on the bonfire around the clock.

3. **Which detail does NOT belong in the oval marked "Soccer Riot"?**

   **A**  The sports fans were well-behaved.

   **B**  This kind of disaster could happen again.

   **C**  Soccer is a popular sport.

   **D**  Organizers were careless in their planning.

**PROVE THE COMPARISON AND CONTRAST** Compare and contrast the two stories by writing brief paragraphs to support the following topic sentences.

In many ways the two stories are alike.

_____

_____

_____

_____

_____

_____

_____

In many ways the two stories are different.

_____

_____

_____

_____

_____

_____

_____

**VERIFYING EVIDENCE** Because a lot of wrong information gets printed, you must verify the accuracy of everything you read. The way to do that is to weigh the evidence presented and decide whether it is trustworthy. Sometimes part of an article may present the correct facts about something, and part of the article may deliberately mislead you. You have to decide whether to believe all or only parts of it. Read the following imaginary testimony from Steven Taljaard, the manager of Ellis Park Stadium in Johannesburg. Then choose the best answer for each question.

[1] I really can't be blamed for what happened. [2] We told the crowd that we were all sold out. [3] But the fans went crazy anyway. [4] They kept pushing and shoving until the fence came down. [5] Soon the situation was out of control. [6] Experts recommend using gas in cases like this, so we tried that. [7] Nothing could calm the crowd. [8] Look, I feel terrible, but you have to hold the fans responsible for their actions.

1. **What evidence is missing from the paragraph?**

   **A** how Taljaard feels

   **B** what kind of gas was used

   **C** how the crowd behaved

   **D** what Taljaard and his staff told the crowd

2. **Which of the following sentences would be most important to verify?**

   **F** Sentence 1

   **G** Sentence 2

   **H** Sentence 6

   **J** Sentence 8

**JUDGE THE EVIDENCE** To persuade the reader of an opinion or story, the author often provides evidence. It is up to the reader to judge if the evidence presented is believable or not.

1. **Which of the following best supports Taljaard's opinion?**

   **A** the previous soccer riot

   **B** a guard's eyewitness account

   **C** someone who listened to the game on the radio

   **D** testimony of a victim's family

2. **Which of the following would be the most convincing in a courtroom?**

   **F** testimony of an expert who warned organizers of possible dangers

   **G** testimony from one of the players

   **H** the 43 death certificates

   **J** Taljaard breaking down into sobs

**PERSUADE WITH EVIDENCE** Write two sentences persuading your reader that not having assigned seats is either dangerous or not dangerous. Be sure to include examples from the stories in this unit to support your answer.

_____

_____

_____

_____

_____

SELECTION 1

# The Tylenol Murders

Twelve-year-old Mary Kellerman didn't feel good. When she woke up in her Chicago-area home on September 29, 1982, she had a runny nose. Her throat was sore. She felt as if she was getting a cold. Her parents gave her an Extra-Strength Tylenol capsule and sent her back to bed. A short time later, Mary Kellerman was dead.

That same morning, not far away, 27-year-old Adam Janus took Extra-Strength Tylenol. He hoped it would ease some minor pain he felt in his chest. An hour later, he collapsed and died.

At first, no one saw a connection between the two deaths. No one knew what had caused these two young people to die. That very night, Adam Janus' family gathered to share their grief. Adam's brother Stanley was stunned and sickened by his brother's death. He felt awful. So he took a Tylenol capsule from a bottle in Adam's home. His wife, Theresa, took one as well. Over the next two days, both Stanley and Theresa became ill and died.

Meanwhile, in another Chicago suburb, 27-year-old Mary Reiner came home after giving birth to her fourth child. She had a headache. So she too took a couple of Tylenol capsules. Like the others, Mary Reiner was soon dead.

In all, seven people from Chicago's West Side died after taking Tylenol for minor aches and pains. It did not take police long to figure out what was going on. But the news was shocking. Someone had put poison into Tylenol capsules. It was the first time in history that this sort of thing had happened.

The police acted quickly. They told people to stop taking Tylenol. And the makers of the product announced a recall. At the time, there were thirty-one million bottles of Tylenol on the market. The company recalled every last one of them.

News of the "Tylenol Murders" led to widespread panic. "Everybody who had Tylenol in the house was frightened," said Chuck Kramer, a rescue worker who had been to the Janus home. One Chicago hospital got seven hundred calls in a single day. And it was not just Chicago. People across the country were gripped with fear. From San Francisco to New Orleans, poison control centers responded to hundreds of frenzied callers.

People took a close look at the products they bought. They saw how easy it was for some madman to tamper with some of them. Pain relievers such as Tylenol had no wrapper. The bottle could be opened right on the shelf. Someone could put in a tainted capsule and then close the bottle again. No one would ever know—until it was too late.

Indeed, the police found tainted Tylenol capsules in a total of eight bottles. All came from stores on Chicago's West Side. All had the same kind of poison—cyanide—in them. But the bottles had different lot numbers. They had come from different plants. So it seemed that the poison had been put in after the capsules left the plants. The police figured that the killer bought or stole the bottles from stores. He or she took them home. The killer emptied the pain medicine out of a few capsules and put in cyanide. The killer then slipped the bottles back onto store shelves when no one was looking.

After a careful review, the police concluded that the killings had been random. None of the victims had been targets. No family members had committed the crime. The killer had struck without knowing whom he or she would kill. It was hard to imagine who would have done such a thing, or why. And despite the best efforts of the police, the killer was never caught.

The makers of Tylenol knew they had to do something to make their product safe again. They began to put safety seals on all their bottles. In fact, they put on *three* seals. Other companies did the same thing. Everything from milk to toothpaste was put into tamper-resistant packages. But "tamper resistant" did not mean "tamper proof." There was just no way to end product-tampering once and for all. And so from time to time, new tragedies occurred.

The next cases came in 1986. That February, Diane Elsroth took two Tylenol capsules. Within minutes, this young New Yorker was dead from cyanide poisoning. In June, a Seattle woman named Sue Snow popped two Excedrin capsules into her mouth. Cyanide killed her, too. And in September, Louis Debner died in his New Jersey home after taking a few sips of Lipton Cup-a-Soup. Once again, cyanide poisoning was the cause of death.

Another death came in 1991. This time the tainted product was the cold remedy Sudafed. The victims were two people in Washington State. The next year it happened again. This time a person died after taking Goody's Headache Powder laced with cyanide.

In some of these cases, the police were able to find the killer. But that was little comfort to the grief-stricken families. And it did not do much to calm the public, either. Each case showed that poison could still be slipped into everyday products. Food and medicine may now come wrapped and sealed and covered. But if someone really wants to poison people, he or she can still find a way to do it.

If you have been timed while reading this article, enter your reading time below. Then turn to the Words-per-Minute Table on page 120 and look up your reading speed (words per minute). Enter your reading speed on the graph on page 121.

**Reading Time:** Selection 1

_____ : _____
MINUTES      SECONDS

**UNDERSTANDING IDEAS** Circle the letter of the best answer.

1. **Which of the following statements about the Tylenol murders is NOT true?**

   A It was the first time that such a thing had happened.

   B There was a killer loose in Chicago.

   C Seven people were poisoned.

   D The seven people were related.

2. **After news of the seven Tylenol deaths was made known,**

   F no new tragedies occurred

   G the killer was caught

   H companies started putting safety seals on products

   J soup was permanently taken off the market

3. **In what way were the experiences of Mary Kellerman and Mary Reiner alike?**

   A They were both careful.

   B They were both poisoned when they took Tylenol.

   C They ignored the warnings.

   D They were from the same family.

4. **When the makers of Tylenol announced a "recall," they**

   F asked the killer to turn himself in

   G took back millions of bottles of Tylenol

   H offered to pay people for buying Tylenol

   J remembered poison being in their factory

**SUMMARIZE** For each blank, choose the word that best completes the meaning of the paragraph.

| | | |
|---|---|---|
| cyanide | poisoned | |
| | | added |
| seals | people | |

For brief periods, in different parts of the country, consumer products like Tylenol turned out to be

_____. These products were

laced with _____. The first such

case was in 1982, in Chicago, where seven

_____ died from taking Tylenol.

Police figured that the cyanide had been

_____ to Tylenol capsules in

stores. Since 1982, many companies have added safety

_____ to their products.

**IF YOU WERE THERE** Write a brief paragraph explaining what you would do if you suspected that a safety seal had been broken. Be sure to include examples from the story in your response.

_____

_____

_____

_____

_____

_____

# Death Through the Mail

"I just couldn't get warm," said Norma Wallace. "I went to my locker at one point to get a sweater, even though I already had one on." The next morning, October 17, 2001, Wallace felt even worse. Finally she went to her doctor. He told her she probably had the flu. The doctor told her to take some Tylenol and return in two days.

"But I got sicker and sicker," Wallace later said. "I was having a lot of trouble breathing and my fever was raging." By the time she went back to the doctor, Wallace could barely walk. This time a team of doctors examined her. They ran several tests. It turned out that Wallace didn't have the flu. She had anthrax. The disease could have killed her. Although it didn't, Wallace did spend eighteen days in the hospital.

Authorities quickly figured out how Wallace got anthrax. She worked as a mail-sorter at a post office center in Trenton, New Jersey. On October 9, when her sorting machine jammed, a mechanic fixed it by blowing away some dust. But this wasn't any old dust. It was a white powder containing spores of anthrax.

An unknown person or persons had mailed letters containing the deadly anthrax spores. Some of the spores had been squeezed out as the letter went through the machine's steel rollers. Whoever mailed the letters had probably been hoping that would happen. He or she apparently wanted to kill anyone who handled or opened the deadly letters.

In a way, Norma Wallace was lucky. Her doctors were on the lookout for anthrax, so they spotted it in time. Fast treatment saved her life. Doctors had been watching for anthrax because several days earlier, on October 5, Robert Stevens had died from the disease. That had set off alarm bells in everyone's mind. Anthrax is an extremely rare disease. Until Robert Stevens became a victim, there had not been a single case of it in the United States in more than twenty-five years. Stevens had been a photo editor for a Florida newspaper. Doctors determined that he had contracted anthrax at work. He had opened an anonymous letter that contained the deadly spores.

Another letter with anthrax was sent to NBC in New York City. This letter went through the sorting center where Norma Wallace worked. And still more letters were sent to members of Congress. These letters went through a sorting center in Washington, D.C.

At first, officials didn't think anthrax spores could be squeezed out of sealed envelopes. So they didn't close the sorting centers that had processed the letters. But then Norma Wallace and other postal workers came down with the disease. The Postal Service finally closed the sorting centers, but it was too late for some employees. Thomas Morris and Joseph Curseen, both workers at the Washington center, died of anthrax inhalation.

News of the anthrax mailings really scared people. It came less than a month after September 11, 2001. On that day, terrorists had hijacked four planes. The terrorists had flown two commercial jets into the World Trade Center in New York City.

Were the anthrax mailings another terrorist attack? No one knew. But the fear was real. "I'm scared to death," admitted one woman. "I think about it constantly. It's all people talk about." Gary Eifried, an expert on terrorism, explained why the anthrax mailings were so terrifying. "Not everyone lives in a tall building or flies on a plane. [But] everyone gets mail."

Robert Greene, a letter carrier in Washington, began wearing rubber gloves and a surgical mask on the job. "Some people don't even want their mail," he said. "I just take it back."

New York City resident Brent Hopkins was one of many who began to dread opening his mail. "I'm definitely scared," Hopkins said. "I get my mail but leave it in a pile and open it every three or four days. I don't really think anyone is going to address any anthrax to me. . . . [But] you never know what's inside until you open it up."

Any strange substance raised suspicions. In Chicago, some people saw some green goo on the sidewalk. They reported it to the police. Before long, a hazardous material unit checked it out. The goo turned out to be guacamole. "Guacamole is not dangerous," said Mayor Richard Daley. "It's good for you. People have to start calming down. I know they are worried. But they can't overreact."

Some people agreed with Mayor Daley. After all, only a few letters had anthrax. The post office handles millions of letters and packages every day. In time, the panic over the mail died down. People started to open their mail less fearfully. Still, fear lingered in the back of their minds. After all, anthrax had killed five people and had made nearly two dozen others very sick. It would be a long time before getting an unexpected letter in the mail would bring anyone joy.

If you have been timed while reading this article, enter your reading time below. Then turn to the Words-per-Minute Table on page 120 and look up your reading speed (words per minute). Enter your reading speed on the graph on page 121.

**Reading Time:** Selection 2

_____ : _____
MINUTES      SECONDS

**UNDERSTANDING IDEAS** Circle the letter of the best answer.

1. **Norma Wallace's tests revealed that she**
   A  had a bad case of the flu
   B  had been exposed to anthrax
   C  could not be cured
   D  failed at her job

2. **Based on the evidence in the story, which statement is NOT true?**
   F  Quick treatment can keep a person from dying from anthrax.
   G  The general public never worried about the anthrax scare.
   H  Postal workers were the hardest hit by the anthrax threat.
   J  There hadn't been a case of anthrax in the U.S. for years.

3. **What conclusion can be reached after reading the story?**
   A  People should stay away from post offices.
   B  It's a good idea to close down the U.S. Postal Service.
   C  Many people thought the anthrax mailings were an act of terrorism.
   D  Anthrax is always fatal.

4. **Why did people become less worried over time?**
   F  No new cases of anthrax were reported.
   G  They got used to threats of terrorism.
   H  They started seeing their doctors more regularly.
   J  The postal service closed all mail sorting centers.

**SUMMARIZE** For each blank, choose the word that best completes the meaning of the paragraph.

| responsible | calm | unexpected |
|---|---|---|
| letters | nation | postal |

Finding anthrax in a few _____

in Trenton, New Jersey, and New York City frightened

an entire _____. After a few

_____ workers died, some people

refused to accept their mail. To this day, no one knows

who was _____ for the anthrax

deaths. Mayor Richard Daley of Chicago told people to try

to stay _____. Still, it took a while

before some people were happy again to get an

_____ letter in the mail.

**IF YOU WERE THERE** If you worked in a post office, what safety measures would you take? Be sure to include examples from the story to support your response.

_____

_____

_____

_____

_____

_____

_____

_____

**USE CONTEXT CLUES** When you read, you may find a word whose meaning is unfamiliar to you. When that happens, you can look up the word's meaning in the dictionary. You can also find out what the word means by looking for context clues. These are words or sentences that come before or after the word. Context clues can be antonyms or synonyms of the unfamiliar word. They may also be an example or definition of the unfamiliar word.

Read each excerpt from the stories you just read. Circle the letter with the best meaning of the underlined word.

1. "People have to start calming down. I know they are worried. But they can't underreact."

   A ignore the situation

   B become easily panicked

   C overlook things

   D relax

2. They saw how easy it was for some madman to tamper with [the packaging]. Pain relievers such as Tylenol had no wrapper. The bottle could be opened right on the shelf.

   F interfere with

   G do something silly

   H alarm people

   J move quickly

3. Doctors determined that he had contracted anthrax at work. He had opened an anonymous letter that contained the deadly spores.

   A signed an agreement

   B become infected with

   C drawn together

   D shortened

4. In time, the panic over the mail died down. People started to open their mail less fearfully. Still, fear lingered in the back of their minds.

   F left

   G increased

   H was erased

   J stayed, remained

5. This time the tainted product was the cold remedy Sudafed. . . . The next year it happened again. This time a person died taking Goody's Headache Powder laced with cyanide.

   A tamper proof

   B contaminated

   C random

   D targeted

**PUT WORDS INTO CONTEXT** Complete the paragraph using the underlined words from the exercise on this page.

The public knows that it is possible for any madman

to _____ with everyday products.

When products are _____ with

poison, they can kill innocent people. However, after

September 11, some people seemed to

_____ to anything strange that they

saw. Reports of postal workers dying because they had

_____ anthrax just added to these

fears. Though fear has _____,

people have continued to live normal lives.

**WORDS THAT COMPARE AND CONTRAST** One type of context clue likens or contrasts an unfamiliar word to a familiar word or concept. When you see words and phrases such as *alike, different, both, also, in contrast, but,* and *yet* you can tell that a comparison or contrast of an unfamiliar term will follow.

For numbers 1 through 8, read the complete paragraph. For each numbered blank, refer to the corresponding number at the right. Choose the compare or contrast word that best completes the meaning of the paragraph.

The 1982 Tylenol murders and the 2001 anthrax mailings are (1) _____ because both resulted in the deaths of unsuspecting people. (2) _____, the way they affected people was quite (3) _____. Here is why. (4) _____, the Tylenol murders were probably the work of a single madman. (5) _____, the anthrax killings may have been related to the major terrorist attack of September 11. People considered (6) _____ incidents to be terrible and tragic. But, (7) _____ the 1982 scare, the anthrax deaths brought with them the threat of widespread terrorism. Do you agree or (8) _____ with this view?

1.  A also
    B same
    C too
    D alike

2.  F Similarly
    G Likewise
    H However
    J Also

3.  A another
    B different
    C separate
    D unlike

4.  F While
    G However
    H On one hand
    J In other ways

5.  A And
    B In contrast
    C Although
    D In other ways

6.  F like
    G same
    H both
    J equal

7.  A like
    B unlike
    C similar
    D equal

8.  F disagree
    G unlike
    H contrast
    J distinct

**ORGANIZE IDEAS** The main ideas in a story are the main topics that are discussed. The specific details are the facts that clarify or support the main ideas. Fill in the chart by using the items listed at the right. If the bulleted item is a main idea from the story, write it in the row marked "Main Idea." If the item is a detail that supports the main idea, write it in the row marked "Detail."

| "The Tylenol Murders" |
| --- |
| **Main Idea:** |
| Detail: |
| Detail: |
| Detail: |
| Detail: |

| "Death Through the Mail" |
| --- |
| **Main Idea:** |
| Detail: |
| Detail: |
| Detail: |
| Detail: |

- Poison control centers got hundreds of calls.
- The bottles were tampered with after they had left the plant.
- People were afraid to open their mail.
- In 1982, seven people died after taking Tylenol laced with cyanide.
- The person or persons responsible for the anthrax letters were never caught.
- A letter laced with anthrax was sent to NBC.
- In 2001, an outbreak of letters contaminated with anthrax spores killed or infected several people.
- The makers of Tylenol recalled every bottle on the market.
- Postal workers started wearing gloves.
- Twelve-year-old Mary Kellerman died after taking Tylenol.

**SUPPORT THE MAIN IDEA** Write a paragraph about contaminated products or items. State the main idea in the first sentence. Then use details from both stories to support your main idea.

_____

_____

_____

_____

_____

_____

**MAKE INFERENCES** Inferences are what the reader learns from what the author has written. When you make an inference, you consider the evidence you've read and then decide what the message is, if it has not already been clearly stated. Circle the letter of the best answer.

1. **What can the reader infer from the following paragraph?**

> After careful review, police concluded that the killings had been random. None of the victims had been targets. No family members had committed the crime.

A The killer knew his victims.

B The killer had no way of knowing who the victims would be.

C Someone was afraid to identify the killer.

D In time, the killer will give himself up.

2. **Which is the best inference a reader can make about the below paragraph?**

> The next morning, October 17, 2001, Wallace felt even worse. Finally she went to her doctor. He told her she probably had the flu. The doctor told her to take some Tylenol and return in two days.

F The doctor was worried about her and told her to come back.

G The doctor knew she had been exposed to anthrax.

H The doctor never suspected anthrax.

J Mary Wallace lost hope.

**APPLY WHAT YOU KNOW**

1. **Read the excerpt from the selection. Why do you think the author put the two phrases in quotes?**

> Everything from milk to toothpaste was put into tamper-resistant packages. But "tamper resistant" did not mean "tamper proof."

A to exaggerate the next cases

B to frighten people

C to call attention to the difference between the two

D to explain what the companies wanted people to know

2. **By saying that "if someone really wants to poison people, he or she can still find a way to do it," the author probably wanted to**

F tell readers to stay away from drugs

G make people worry

H show that the threat still exists in spite of safety measures

J show how crazy people act

**JUDGE THE EVIDENCE** Write a brief paragraph stating if you believe people should be concerned about being poisoned. Support your opinion with evidence from the stories in this unit.

_____

_____

_____

_____

_____

_____

# Heart Attack!

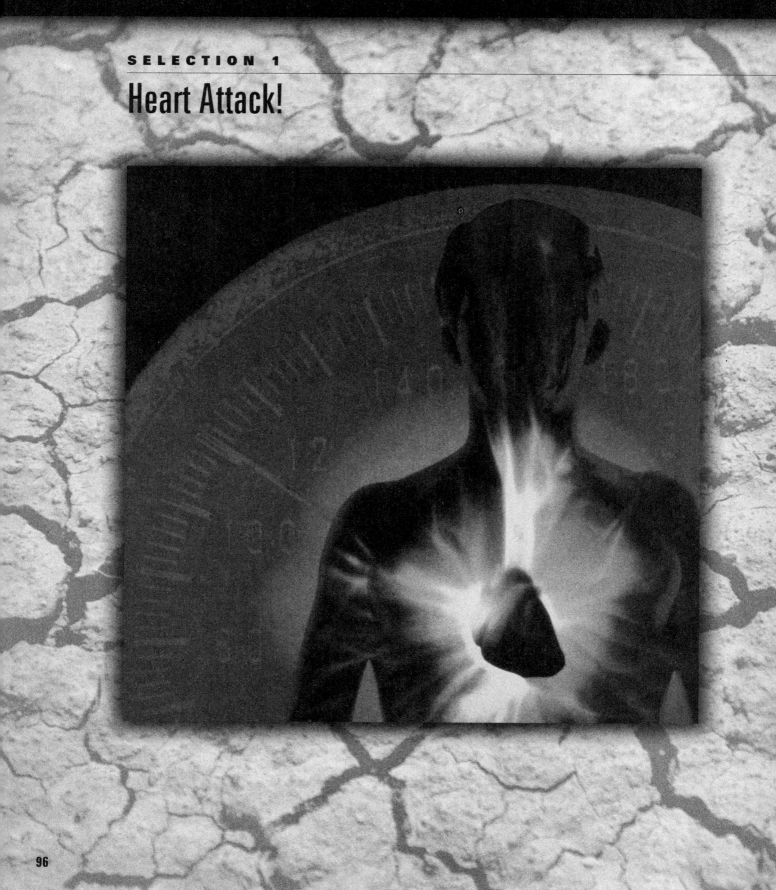

It sounded like a bad joke, but David Phillips wasn't kidding. According to him, the number "four" could literally scare people to death. Or, to be more specific, it could scare Chinese Americans and Japanese Americans to death.

Phillips was a researcher at the University of San Diego. One day a student explained to him that the number four was considered unlucky in Chinese and Japanese culture. That's because in China and Japan, the word *four* is pronounced just like the word *death*. Phillips was intrigued. He was interested to learn that in China and Japan, hotels don't use the number four when they number their rooms. Neither do hospitals. Even the Chinese air force avoids putting that number on its planes.

"I have often wondered if people could indeed die of fright, and, if so, how this could be investigated quantitatively," said Phillips. This seemed to be his chance to find out. He figured that if the number four caused people distress, they might be more likely to have heart attacks on the fourth day of the month than on any other day.

Armed with this idea, Phillips went to work. He checked forty-seven million death certificates from the years 1973 to 1998. He noted the death rate for different groups. And he took special notice of those who had died from heart attacks. What he found amazed him. Asian Americans died from heart attacks at a much higher rate on the fourth of each month than on any other day. On that unlucky day, their death rate went up 13 percent.

Phillips' study was reported in the *British Medical Journal* in December of 2001. Some people dismissed his findings as a coincidence. They pointed out that European Americans think of the number "13" as unlucky. Yet the death rate for these people doesn't go up on the 13th of the month. Others, however, thought Phillips' study was important. They felt it helped show how stress and fear can affect people's bodies. After all, studies have indicated that the chances of having a heart attack are greatest on Monday mornings. That seems to be related to the stress of returning to work after a weekend off.

If the number four or the thought of facing another Monday morning can lead to a heart attack, imagine what something really frightful can do. Think of a war or an earthquake. Can such events scare people to death? Some studies have suggested they can. Take a look at the Persian Gulf War of 1991. Israel faced the threat of mass destruction by Iraq. Tension ran high among many Israelis. Everyone was given a gas mask. Everyone was given medicine in case of a chemical attack. And every family was urged to prepare a sealed room at home.

The war began on January 17. The next day Iraq fired missiles into Israel. The heart attack rate in Israel that day jumped dramatically. One hundred and forty-seven Israelis died on the first day of the attacks. (No one died from a missile hit.) The normal rate was ninety-three deaths. So this was a 58 percent increase. In Tel Aviv and Haifa, the two main targets, the death rate jumped 80 percent.

Earthquakes have caused the same reaction. On January 17, 1994, an earthquake struck Northridge, California. The quake killed fifty-one people. Most died as a direct result of the earthquake damage. They died when buildings crumbled or elevated highways collapsed. About twenty people, however, died from heart attacks.

One terrified woman felt her house shake. Then the shaking stopped. There was no damage to her house. But the woman herself kept shaking with fear. She felt a pain in her chest. She had trouble breathing. Realizing that she was in trouble, the woman tried to dial 911.

There was no dial tone. The earthquake had knocked out the phone lines. A few minutes later, the woman died of a heart attack.

Another victim was found in his car. He had escaped his swaying house, but he couldn't outrun his fear. He had died from a heart attack while sitting in the safety of his car. Many other people made it to the hospital only to have their hearts give out once they got there.

Most people, of course, can survive a great deal of stress. They don't die because war is declared or an earthquake hits. They don't die when the fourth of the month rolls around or when the sun rises on a Monday morning. But for some people, especially those with weak hearts, stress or sudden fear can be a killer. These people, it seems, really can be scared to death.

If you have been timed while reading this article, enter your reading time below. Then turn to the Words-per-Minute Table on page 120 and look up your reading speed (words per minute). Enter your reading speed on the graph on page 121.

**Reading Time:** Selection 1

_____ : _____
MINUTES        SECONDS

**UNDERSTANDING IDEAS** Circle the letter of the best answer.

1. **Why do Chinese and Japanese hotels avoid using the number four on doors?**

   **A** The number four is pronounced like the word *death*.

   **B** Most hotels are too small to have more than three rooms.

   **C** The number four is not as well liked as the number five.

   **D** The number four is hard to read.

2. **David Phillips' study proves that**

   **F** Israelis have more heart attacks than Asians

   **G** stress can seriously affect people's bodies

   **H** death rates decrease when people go to war

   **J** all of the above

3. **Based on the evidence in the story, which of the following does NOT add to stress?**

   **A** earthquakes

   **B** fear

   **C** war

   **D** the number 13

4. **The fact that Phillips checked 47 million death certificates proves that he was**

   **F** determined to check his theory

   **G** avoiding taking a trip to China

   **H** anxious to avoid having a heart attack

   **J** hoping hotels would start using the number four again

**SUMMARIZE** For each blank, choose the word that best completes the meaning of the paragraph.

| stressful | death | day |
|-----------|-------|-----|
| frighten | fourth | heart |

The number four can actually

_____ a person to death!

In China and Japan the word for *four* is pronounced

like the word for *death*. There is a higher

_____ rate in those two countries

on the _____ day of each month

than on any other _____. Fear of

war, earthquakes, or anything _____

can also cause _____ attacks and

even death.

**IF YOU WERE THERE** What would you do if someone you cared about was under a lot of stress? Be sure to include examples from the story to support your response.

_____

_____

_____

_____

_____

_____

# One Scary Man

John Waldie killed two people—sort of. He didn't mean to kill them. But as the headline in *The Herald of Scotland* put it on May 16, 1998, they were both "scared to death." The *Scotsman* echoed that claim, describing one of the victims as "frightened to death."

Waldie's first victim was Rose McCrudden. The 82-year-old widow lived alone in an apartment in Leith, Scotland. McCrudden had a history of heart trouble. She also suffered from senility. Often she forgot that her beloved husband was dead, and she sat by the window waiting for him to return from the store.

John Waldie lived nearby and knew the elderly Mrs. McCrudden. Early in the morning of July 1, 1992, Waldie broke into her apartment, intending to rob her. He expected McCrudden to be asleep, but she wasn't. When McCrudden ran into him in a hallway, she was so scared she suffered a heart attack.

This wasn't what Waldie had planned. He panicked. Carrying McCrudden to her bed, he tried frantically to revive her. He tried mouth-to-mouth resuscitation and CPR. It didn't work. After ten frenzied minutes, he fled the apartment.

Waldie felt guilty for what he had done. Hours later, he made an anonymous call for an ambulance. He hoped she might still be alive, but she wasn't. In fact, by the time Waldie made his telephone call, McCrudden's dead body had already been discovered. A neighbor had become worried when the elderly lady didn't open her curtains in the morning. The neighbor had called McCrudden's son, who came to the apartment and found his mother lying lifeless in bed.

Police traced the anonymous ambulance call. That led them straight to John Waldie, whom they quickly charged with murder. Doctors later discovered that McCrudden had died from a combination of things. Stark terror and heart failure played a big part. According to doctors, she also suffered a broken rib when Waldie tried to revive her.

Waldie maintained that he had not intended to harm McCrudden. "I never killed her," he protested. "I thought she was already dead. She collapsed after seeing me. I was only helping."

No one bought that excuse. But the court didn't find Waldie guilty of murder. Instead, Judge Lord Caplan found him guilty of a lesser charge—culpable homicide. Lord Caplan sentenced Waldie to seven years in prison. "You broke into the house of an elderly lady you knew was frail in health for the purpose of stealing from her," he scolded Waldie.

"That is a despicable action in itself. If you had not broken into this house, there is a possibility that the lady [would still be] alive."

By 1997, Waldie was out of prison. But he wasn't out of trouble. On December 27 of that year, he got into an argument with Terry Kivlin. The two men were drinking together in a pub when they started arguing. At one point Kivlin assaulted Waldie. Despite this, Waldie invited Kivlin back to his apartment. Once there, Waldie offered Kivlin a drink and told him to make himself at home.

A third man, Ronnie Smith, also happened to be in the apartment, and he witnessed what happened next. For reasons that weren't clear, Waldie grew angry with Kivlin. Waldie disappeared into the kitchen and returned swinging a club made from the leg of a coffee table. Waldie hit Kivlin with the club. He also shouted and swore at him. Apparently, Waldie's actions terrified Kivlin. Kivlin dashed to a window, climbed out, and fell seven stories to his death.

The police arrested Waldie. Once again, Waldie expressed remorse about what had happened, but insisted that he was not guilty of murder. After all, he hadn't pushed Kivlin out of the window. On the other hand, he had created so much fear in Kivlin that the man jumped to his death. For the second time, a court found Waldie guilty of culpable homicide.

The judge had a hard time deciding what sentence to hand down. He could have sent Waldie to prison for a very long time. Addressing Waldie, he pointed out that this was the second time "your frightening conduct has led to a death." But the judge noted that Kivlin had attacked Waldie earlier in the evening. He also acknowledged that Kivlin's fall "from the seventh floor was never contemplated by you for a moment." In the end, the judge sentenced Waldie to five years in prison.

Kivlin's relatives were angered by what they perceived to be too light a sentence. Ken Marr, Kivlin's brother-in-law, said, "We are very, very upset at the sentence. It's a disgrace."

If you have been timed while reading this article, enter your reading time below. Then turn to the Words-per-Minute Table on page 120 and look up your reading speed (words per minute). Enter your reading speed on the graph on page 121.

**Reading Time:** Selection 2

_____ : _____
MINUTES       SECONDS

## UNDERSTANDING IDEAS Circle the letter of the best answer.

1. **The fact that John Waldie tried to help Rose McCrudden proves that he**

   A  knew her

   B  had not meant to harm her

   C  deserved to have all charges dropped

   D  was more kind-hearted than her neighbor

2. **What did Terry Kivlin and John Waldie have in common?**

   F  They lived in the same neighborhood.

   G  They both had been to jail.

   H  They both had been in trouble before.

   J  Each had attacked the other.

3. **What did Ronnie Smith observe?**

   A  Waldie's actions scared Kivlin enough that he went out the window.

   B  Kivlin committed suicide.

   C  The judge made an error in sentencing.

   D  Waldie pushed Kivlin out of the window.

4. **According to the story, why were Kivlin's relatives angry?**

   F  They hadn't been able to say good-bye to Kivlin.

   G  They thought Ronnie Smith should also be punished.

   H  They believed that Waldie deserved a harsher sentence.

   J  They thought Waldie deserved to go free.

## SUMMARIZE For each blank, choose the word that best completes the meaning of the paragraph.

| attack | prison | jumped |
|--------|--------|--------|
| scare  | rob    | kill   |

If it is possible to _____ people to death, John Waldie did it twice. First, he frightened an elderly lady when he broke into her apartment to _____ her. When she saw Waldie in her apartment, the woman had a heart _____ and died. Waldie went to _____ for seven years for the crime. When he got out, he frightened Terry Kivlin so badly that Kivlin _____ seven stories to his death. Two people had died, though Waldie had never meant to _____ anyone.

## IF YOU WERE THERE Write a brief paragraph explaining what you think is a fair sentence for Waldie. Be sure to include examples from the story to support your response.

_____

_____

_____

_____

_____

_____

**USE CONTEXT CLUES** When you read, you may find a word whose meaning is unfamiliar to you. When that happens, you can look up the word's meaning in the dictionary. You can also find out what the word means by looking for context clues. These are words or sentences that come before or after the word. Context clues can be antonyms or synonyms of the unfamiliar word. They may also be an example or definition of the unfamiliar word.

Read each excerpt from the stories you just read. Circle the letter with the best meaning of the underlined word.

1. **The police arrested Waldie. Once again, Waldie expressed remorse about what had happened, but insisted that he was not guilty of murder.**

   **A** begged to be free

   **B** caused to move fast

   **C** showed, or put into words

   **D** made an excuse

2. **"I have often wondered if people could indeed die of fright, and if so, how this could be investigated quantitatively," said Phillips. . . . He checked forty-seven million death certificates from the years 1973 to 1998.**

   **F** easily determined without counting

   **G** absolutely

   **H** proved with numbers and facts

   **J** with great effort

3. **But the court didn't find Waldie guilty of murder. Instead, Judge Lord Caplan found him guilty of a lesser charge—culpable homicide. Lord Caplan sentenced Waldie to seven years in prison.**

   **A** blameworthy

   **B** friendly

   **C** innocent

   **D** evil

4. **"You broke into the house of an elderly lady you knew was in frail health for the purpose of stealing from her," he scolded Waldie. "That is a despicable action in itself."**

   **F** annoying

   **G** horrible

   **H** friendly

   **J** able to make happen immediately

5. **But the judge noted that Kivlin had attacked Waldie earlier in the evening. He also acknowledged that Kivlin's fall "from the seventh floor was never contemplated by you for a moment." In the end, the judge sentenced Waldie to five years in prison.**

   **A** expected

   **B** suprised by

   **C** thought about, considered

   **D** feared

**PUT WORDS INTO CONTEXT** Complete the paragraph using the underlined words from the exercise on this page.

David Phillips had a way to prove

_____ that people could die of fright.

People who dismissed his findings probably had not heard

of John Waldie of Scotland. Two years earlier, he had

been found _____ for contributing to

the deaths of two people. In both cases, Waldie's actions

were _____. But each time Waldie

_____ remorse for what had

happened. Each time he explained that he had never

meant to kill anyone.

**PREFIXES AND SUFFIXES** As you have learned, one way of finding out the meaning of a word is by looking at prefixes and suffixes, the letters that are added to either the beginning or the end of a word to change its meaning. For example, the prefix *il-* means *not*. So the word *illegal* means "not legal." The suffix *–ness* means "a state or condition." So the word *illness* means "the condition of being ill."

Use a dictionary to find the meaning of each prefix or suffix below. Match the prefix or suffix with its meaning on the right. Examples for each definition are included in italics. Write the letter of the correct definition on the line. **One letter is used twice.**

_____ **1.** un-

_____ **2.** -ful

_____ **3.** dis-

_____ **4.** -er

_____ **5.** re-

_____ **6.** -ly

**A** prefix: the opposite of, not: *unhappy, disinterest*

**B** suffix: characterized by, full of: *careful*

**C** suffix: in the manner of, like: *slowly*

**D** suffix: a person who: *teacher*

**E** prefix: again: *replay*

**WRITE DEFINITIONS** On the line next to each word from the story, write the new meaning of the word with the added prefix or suffix.

**1.** dis + appear = disappear

definition: _____

**2.** un + lucky = unlucky

definition: _____

**3.** quiet + ly = quietly

definition: _____

**4.** fright + ful = frightful

definition: _____

**5.** research + er = researcher

definition: _____

**6.** re + wind = rewind

definition: _____

**7.** un + safe = unsafe

definition: _____

**ORGANIZE THE FACTS** To understand a passage, you should ask questions about the text before, during, and after reading and then look for answers. Sometimes the answer might be stated directly in the passage; other times you need to put ideas or information together to come up with the answer. Sometimes the answer may not be in the passage at all, but may be what you already know.

Look at the chart below. Then answer the questions on the right.

| Question-Answer Relationships | |
| --- | --- |
| **Question** | **How to Answer** |
| • Who was accused of scaring two people to death? | Question words such as *who*, *where*, and *when* usually indicate that the answer is right there in the passage. |
| • What caused some people to dismiss David Phillip's claim that people could die of fright? | The question words *what* and *why* sometimes require you to think and to search the passage. |
| • Why is a lot of stress dangerous for some people? | A general question like this is about something you probably know. You can come up with the answer on your own. |
| • How do you think people are most likely to react if Phillips published a study about the number 13? | A question that asks for what you think requires you to use what you already know and what the author tells you to draw an inference or a conclusion. |

1. **Which question can you answer by looking for a direct statement from the story?**

   A What evidence did the judge weigh in sentencing Waldie?

   B Why did Waldie feel bad about McCrudden's death?

   C How do you think McCrudden's relatives must have felt?

   D Who caused Rose McCrudden's death?

2. **Which question can you answer by thinking and searching?**

   F When was Phillips' study published?

   G What made Phillips think that Asians didn't like the number four?

   H Where did John Waldie live?

   J How do you think Waldie should be punished?

3. **Which question requires you to use what you already know from experience and what the author tells you?**

   A What caused Rose McCudden's death?

   B Who was Ronnie Smith?

   C How do you think a jury should have voted at Waldie's trial?

   D Where did Rose McCrudden live?

**WRITE YOUR OWN QUESTIONS** Write two questions about each of the stories in this unit. For each question, explain how you would find the answer.

_____

_____

_____

_____

_____

**FACT AND OPINION** Facts and opinions can sometimes be hard to tell apart. People often represent an opinion as if it were a fact. To tell if something is a fact or an opinion, determine whether what is being said is something that can be proven to be true. If it can, it's a fact. If it states what someone thinks or how someone feels, it's an opinion. Read the following passage about the number 13. Then choose the best answer to each question.

[1] Scandinavians believed that the number 13 meant bad luck. [2] According to old myths, there were 13 gods. [3] One of these gods was named Loki. [4] They believed Loki was an evil, cruel god who brought misfortune to humans. [5] This is just a silly superstition. [6] It comes from beliefs people used to explain events that were beyond their control. [7] Today's beliefs will become tomorrow's superstitions.

1. **Which sentence does NOT state a fact?**

   A  Sentence 1

   B  Sentence 2

   C  Sentence 3

   D  Sentence 5

2. **Which sentence from the passage states an opinion?**

   F  Sentence 2

   G  Sentence 3

   H  Sentence 4

   J  Sentence 7

**JUDGE THE EVIDENCE** To convince a reader to agree to an opinion, the writer often provides evidence. The reader has to judge if the evidence is adequate to support the opinion. Choose the best answer.

1. **Which statement best supports the opinion that people can die from stress?**

   A  The heart attack rate in Israel jumped 58% at the start of the Persian Gulf War.

   B  On January 17, 1994, an earthquake killed 51 people.

   C  In the end, the judge sentenced Waldie to five years in prison.

   D  Hotels in China and Japan don't use four when they number their rooms.

2. **Which statement best supports the opinion that most people can survive a great deal of stress?**

   F  For people with weak hearts, sudden fear can be a killer.

   G  The amount of heart attacks doesn't always increase in times of war or natural disasters.

   H  The highest risk period for heart attacks is Monday mornings.

   J  Waldie panicked but took the time to perform CPR on Rose McCrudden.

**YOUR OPINION** Write a brief paragraph expressing your opinion about the causes of sudden heart attacks. Support your opinion with evidence from the stories you have read.

_____

_____

_____

_____

_____

# FEARS OF THE MIND

SELECTION 1

## Don't Box Me In

As a star soccer player in England, Ian Wright was known for his scoring skills and his rough play. Opponents feared and respected him.

But if Wright were put in any enclosed space, he turned into a very frightened man. He detested flying on airplanes. "I start looking round the cabin and I feel trapped," he once said. "I just sit there paranoid, looking at my wife and kids and thinking, 'We're all going to die.'"

Like millions of other people, Wright had claustrophobia. This phobia is an extreme fear of enclosed places. Sufferers feel trapped in airplanes, elevators, and other tight spots. When that happens, these people usually panic. They grow lightheaded and start breathing faster. Their heart rate accelerates rapidly and they may begin shaking. Some sufferers even faint or become sick.

Wright had a severe case of claustrophobia. He couldn't ride in a subway train without trepidation. He had an even greater fear of going up or down in an elevator. "I just get anxious and want to get off," he said. "I can't stand it. This terrible feeling of panic and doom comes over me and I feel physically ill. I imagine we're going to go crashing down to the bottom of the elevator shaft."

Wright realized that his fear was irrational. In his mind, he knew that the elevator was probably not going to crash. Still, he couldn't shake the gut feeling that it would. "I know in my heart of hearts that logically it probably will not happen," he said, "but when I get the panic, nothing can convince me otherwise."

Tracey Moulton was so claustrophobic that she never closed her bathroom door. It didn't matter who else was around, either. She said, "If you put me in a public restroom, there's no way I'd lock the cubicle door."

People can become claustrophobic at any time in their lives. Some of them don't know how or why they came to fear tight spaces. Others can point to a specific incident that triggered a lifetime of fear. For Moulton, that incident occurred when she was a child. Her father took her to a hospital to pick up her mother, who was a patient there. While at the hospital, Moulton got stuck all by herself in an elevator. "I was totally panic-stricken," she recalled. "It felt like the elevator was taking me away from my mother, kidnapping me. After that, I would break out in a sweat every time I went in an elevator."

By the time Moulton was seventeen, her fear of elevators caused her so much distress that she avoided riding in them altogether. She took the stairs instead.

However, that didn't solve her problem. Her fear soon spread to other enclosed places. Moulton grew to hate the subway. "When I'm on an underground platform, I have palpitations," she said.

Moulton once got stuck on a subway train for about an hour. She was so scared it almost drove her mad. "When I got off, I charged up the stairs and burst into tears," she admitted.

Bebe Moore Campbell also suffered from claustrophobia. She found it difficult to ride in elevators in Los Angeles' high-rise buildings. Campbell explained, "When I enter an elevator, especially an empty one, and watch the doors close, I feel like letting loose a wild, primal scream of terror."

But she usually didn't. That was because Campbell had her own bag of tricks for dealing with her fear. When riding in an elevator, she might close her eyes and dream of lying on a beach in some faraway land. Or she might count backwards from 100. She might tell herself a joke or recite favorite passages she had memorized from the Bible.

In early 2001, however, those tricks were not enough. California began to suffer from an energy shortage. Every now and then, the power would go off. During these blackouts, elevators ground to a halt. Campbell felt that the odds of getting stuck in a darkened elevator were suddenly much higher. "In Los Angeles, elevators really could stop anytime, anywhere," she said.

So Campbell began walking up as many as twenty-five flights of stairs to avoid getting into an elevator. She tried to put a positive spin on this by calling it her new exercise program. And Campbell pointed out that she wasn't alone. Other people were also taking the stairs. "There are a lot of Americans who suffer from panic disorders," she said. "When faced with the object we dread, we sweat, our hearts pound, we feel as though we are losing our minds. And when the onslaught is over, our greatest fear is that it will happen again."

Despite the tears and fears, there is good news. There is hope for people who suffer from claustrophobia. Doctors offer all sorts of treatments, from psychological therapies to drugs. But first, sufferers need to follow the example set by Ian Wright, Tracey Moulton, and Bebe Moore Campbell. Although difficult, they admitted they had a problem. As one expert put it, "It's hard for adults to admit that they are scared out of their wits or helpless to control their fears."

If you have been timed while reading this article, enter your reading time below. Then turn to the Words-per-Minute Table on page 120 and look up your reading speed (words per minute). Enter your reading speed on the graph on page 121.

**Reading Time:** Selection 1

_____ : _____
MINUTES      SECONDS

**UNDERSTANDING IDEAS** Circle the letter of the best answer.

1. **What was Ian Wright's greatest fear?**

   A his wife and kids knowing what was on his mind

   B panic attacks

   C being trapped in closed, tight places

   D not scoring well in soccer

2. **Which statement about claustrophobia is TRUE?**

   F A person can develop claustrophobia at any point in life.

   G People develop claustrophobia from spending too much time in cars.

   H Fear of air travel is a claustrophobic's biggest fear.

   J There is no treatment for claustrophobia.

3. **Symptoms of a panic disorder include**

   A pounding heart

   B light-headedness

   C sweating

   D all of the above

4. **Based on evidence in the story, readers can conclude that**

   F fears can never be overcome

   G all panic attacks date back to early incidents in life

   H there is no hope for people who suffer from claustrophobia

   J there are treatments to help people deal with claustrophobia

**SUMMARIZE** For each blank, choose the word that best completes the meaning of the paragraph.

| fears | closed | |
|-------|--------|--------|
| soccer | claustrophobic | elevator |

Ian Wright is a famous _____ star in England. He also suffers from claustrophobia. Similarly, Tracey Moulton is _____ and avoids tight or _____ places at all costs. Other people, like Bebe Moore Campbell, try to deal with their _____. When Bebe is in an _____, she imagines herself lying on a beach.

**IF YOU WERE THERE** If you suffered from claustrophobia, what coping strategies would you try? Explain your answer in a brief paragraph. Be sure to include examples from the story to support your response.

# Leave Me Alone

"When I was young I never wanted to go to birthday parties," Sarah Brookes said. "I didn't know how to mix and found it difficult talking to other kids." As Brookes grew older, her fears became more exaggerated. She hated being in any situation that could cause her embarrassment. As she admitted, "I couldn't go up to a shop assistant to ask a question because I was frightened of saying something stupid."

Brookes' fears developed into full-blown agoraphobia, or fear of public places. Agoraphobia is the most common of all phobias. A person with a mild case fears certain situations but can usually cope with them. Anyone with a moderate case tries to avoid situations that cause discomfort. For example, he or she might stay away from popular sporting events or crowded supermarkets. But a person with a severe case of agoraphobia might never want to leave the house. He or she dreads being around new people and can't stand any situation that threatens to get out of control. For Sarah Brookes, the "safe" zone didn't extend past her front door.

On July 27, 2002, Jenny Ellis wrote a newspaper article describing what it was like to live with agoraphobia. Ellis had a particularly severe case, and she began her article with a scary confession. "On November 15 this year it will be exactly seven years since I've set foot outside," she wrote. "The thought of leaving the house has me fighting for breath, terrified at what's out there."

Kaye Machin also had an extreme case of agoraphobia. It developed when she was eighteen years old. One day she headed out for a walk, but had to stop after only a few steps. "A sudden fear and panic came over me," she recalled. "It felt as though everything was falling in on me, even though I was out in the open air." Machin continued for about six hundred feet, but eventually the panic became too great. "I had to knock on a stranger's door and ask her to walk me to my [home]. I had no idea what was happening to me."

Machin endured such attacks for the next twenty-five years. Once she stayed in her house for six years without ever leaving. She moved back in with her parents, but that didn't really help. She spent two years refusing to leave her bedroom. "I was not living," she said. "I was like a shadow. I couldn't stand to look at the outside world and see daytime."

After many years of struggle, Machin's condition finally did improve. Although she wasn't fully cured, she learned to face her fears. "Even when I feel dreadfully ill," she said, "I know I can go out and hang the washing on the line or go through doorways. At one time I couldn't do that. I intend to get a little better every single day."

Agoraphobia almost ruined Vince Van Patten's life. In the early 1980s, Van Patten was a rising tennis star, regularly beating some of the best players in the game. But by 1985, he had developed an intense and irrational fear of people, including his fans.

"It started on the court," he explained. "Then I got to the point where I basically wanted to stay in one place and couldn't be in any kind of pressure situation or public place without feeling this anxiety." Whenever he did venture out, Van Patten became sweaty and lightheaded. "I thought I was going nuts," he said.

Van Patten's doctor prescribed powerful drugs, but Van Patten didn't want to become dependent on medication, so he stopped using them after a few days. Instead he began reading all he could about agoraphobia. He also prayed a lot. It took two hard years, but Van Patten slowly improved.

"I got strength from somewhere and helped myself through that power," he said. "Now I feel 100 percent better."

Jenny Ellis wasn't so fortunate. The fear that gripped her wouldn't let go. "Even the thought of putting the washing out leaves people like me in a state of severe panic," she wrote. "I sit in the same chair, in the same room, day after day, paralyzed by fear. My life is ruled by an invisible demon who waits for me in the outside world."

Ellis recalled the day she summoned all her courage and attempted to go out on a shopping expedition. When she turned the lock to open the front door, she was overcome with fear. "I staggered to the bathroom, where I collapsed on the floor," she said. "I couldn't swallow and my tongue and arms felt numb."

That attack passed but the phobia remained. "I hope one day I will find the strength to break free," she wrote. "Until then I can only wait."

If you have been timed while reading this article, enter your reading time below. Then turn to the Words-per-Minute Table on page 120 and look up your reading speed (words per minute). Enter your reading speed on the graph on page 121.

**Reading Time:** Selection 2

_____ : _____
MINUTES      SECONDS

**UNDERSTANDING IDEAS** Circle the letter of the best answer.

**1. Which of the following statements is TRUE?**

 **A** Agoraphobia is a fear of public places.

 **B** People with severe cases may never leave home.

 **C** Agoraphobia is the most common phobia.

 **D** all of the above

**2. What did Kaye Machin and Jenny Ellis have in common?**

 **F** They both lived with their parents.

 **G** They made sure that they had company at all times.

 **H** They gave up all hope.

 **J** They became paralyzed with fear when they left their homes.

**3. How did Van Patten's experience differ from those of Machin and Ellis?**

 **A** He took several drugs.

 **B** He had the support of his fans.

 **C** He was able to get over his agoraphobia.

 **D** Doctors were able to help him.

**4. All of the following are examples of things an agoraphobic would avoid EXCEPT**

 **F** a sports stadium

 **G** a crowded shopping mall

 **H** watching TV on the couch at home

 **J** taking a walk on the street

**SUMMARIZE** For each blank, choose the word that best completes the meaning of the paragraph.

| | | |
|---|---|---|
| stranger | public | walk |
| years | severe | |

People who suffer from _____ agoraphobia spend all their time at home. They are afraid to go out, meet people, or be seen in _____. Jenny Ellis did not set foot outside her door for seven _____. Kaye Machlin developed agoraphobia at age 18 when she went out for a _____. She had to ask a _____ to help her get home.

**IF YOU WERE THERE** Imagine that you started to feel very uncomfortable in public places. Write a brief paragraph explaining what you would do. Be sure to include examples from the story to support your response.

_____

_____

_____

_____

_____

_____

_____

**USE CONTEXT CLUES** When you read, you may find a word whose meaning is unfamiliar to you. When that happens, you can look up the word's meaning in the dictionary. You can also find out what the word means by looking for context clues. These are words or sentences that come before or after the word. Context clues can be antonyms or synonyms of the unfamiliar word. They may also be an example or definition of the unfamiliar word.

Read each excerpt from the stories you just read. Circle the letter with the best meaning of the underlined word.

1. **They grow lightheaded and start breathing faster. Their heart rate underline{accelerates} rapidly and they may begin shaking.**

   **A** increases

   **B** drops

   **C** becomes uneven

   **D** pounds

2. **[Wright] couldn't ride in a subway train without trepidation. He had an even greater fear of going up and down in an elevator.**

   **F** help

   **G** fear or dread

   **H** exhaustion

   **J** medication

3. **Wright realized that his fear was irrational. In his mind, he knew the elevator was probably not going to crash.**

   **A** irresponsible

   **B** funny

   **C** unreasonable

   **D** not able to move

4. **Ellis recalled the day she summoned all her courage and attempted to go out on a shopping expedition.**

   **F** product bought at the mall

   **G** trip made for a specific reason

   **H** experiment

   **J** occasion

5. **Machin endured such attacks for the next twenty-five years. . . . "I was like a shadow. I couldn't stand to look at the outside world and see daytime."**

   **A** put up with

   **B** fought off

   **C** continued

   **D** imagined

**PUT WORDS INTO CONTEXT** Complete the paragraph using the underlined words from the exercise on this page.

Agoraphobia is the fear of public places. Some people have _____ severe panic attacks at the thought of leaving home. They become filled with _____. Their palms become sweaty. Their heart rate _____. They may become sick and light-headed just thinking about taking a short shopping _____. Knowing that their fears are _____ does not help these people. But time and hard work offer hope of getting better.

**MAKE ROOT CONNECTIONS** One way of finding out the meaning of a word is by looking for its root. An unfamiliar word may share a common root with a word that you know. A root is a part of many different words and may not be a word by itself. The root *aster* or *astro* comes from a Greek word that means "star." You will find the root in words like *asteroid* and *astronomy*.

Look for the root that connects each group of words. Then choose the best meaning of the root.

1. **expedition, pedal, pedestrian**
   - A foot
   - B street
   - C fast
   - D journey

2. **psychological, psychiatry, psychosomatic**
   - F ridiculous or silly
   - G complicated
   - H of the mind, soul, or spirit
   - J homemade

3. **public, publicity, publication**
   - A people
   - B extraordinary
   - C medicine
   - D view

4. **agoraphobia, arachnophobia, xenophobia**
   - F fear
   - G strangers
   - H medicine
   - J doctors

5. **invisible, vision, visibility**
   - A proving
   - B showing
   - C seeing
   - D visiting

6. **irrational, rationale, rationalize**
   - F limit
   - G search
   - H reason or understanding
   - J having worth

**ROOT ANALOGIES** Analogies show similar patterns and relationships between words. Root analogies show relationships between words that have the same root word. For example, *use* is to *useable* as *move* is to *moveable*. Both root words, when combined with *able*, make a new word. For each blank, choose a root word from the exercise on this page to correctly complete the analogy. Not all of the words will be used.

1. *improve* is to *prove* as *xenophobia* is to

   _____.

2. *prediction* is to *dict* as *invisible* is to

   _____.

3. *psychological* is to *psycho* as *publication* is to

   _____.

4. *pedestrian* is to *ped* as *psychology* is to

   _____.

5. *publicity* is to *public* as *rationalize* is to

   _____.

**ORGANIZE THE FACTS** The two stories you read in this unit are alike in some ways and different in other ways. A Venn diagram can show how they are alike and different. Look at the Venn diagram below. Then choose the best answer to each question.

"DON'T BOX ME IN"
Claustrophobia

BOTH
Strong fear

"LEAVE ME ALONE"
Agoraphobia

1. **Which of the following details belongs in the oval marked BOTH?**

   **A** panic attacks

   **B** fear of closed places

   **C** fear of public places

   **D** no chance of recovery

2. **Which detail does NOT belong in the oval marked BOTH?**

   **F** doctors can prescribe drugs

   **G** fear of small spaces

   **H** sudden fear and panic

   **J** light-headedness, sweating

3. **Which detail does NOT belong in the oval marked "Don't Box Me In"?**

   **A** The people feared riding in elevators.

   **B** Doctors offered many treatments.

   **C** They struggled for years.

   **D** They could not be in public places.

4. **Which detail does NOT belong in the oval marked "Leave Me Alone"?**

   **F** stayed away from crowds

   **G** felt trapped at home

   **H** didn't feel safe in public places

   **J** did not seek out new experiences

**PROVE THE COMPARISON AND CONTRAST** Compare and contrast the two stories by writing brief paragraphs that support the topic sentences below.

In many ways the two stories are alike.

In many ways the two stories are different.

**DRAW CONCLUSIONS** You draw conclusions every day. You make judgments based on the information available to you. If you see a traffic jam when you get onto the highway, you may conclude that there is construction work or an accident. You may take an alternate route, or you may stay on the highway, depending on how much time you have. In big and little ways, you draw your own conclusions all the time. Read the following paragraph about phobias and then choose the best answer to each question.

[1] Phobias can seriously affect a person's quality of life. [2] It is not uncommon for phobic people to avoid what they fear at all costs. [3] Claustrophobics may climb 25 flights of stairs to avoid getting into an elevator. [4] Agoraphobics may not be able to leave their homes for years. [5] Knowing what one fears does not necessarily help a phobic person control or overcome that fear.

1. **Which conclusion can you draw based on the paragraph above?**
   A People with phobias feel overpowered by their fears.
   B People with phobias can lead normal lives.
   C People with phobias would benefit from support groups.
   D Phobias do not last longer than a week.

2. **Which sentence supports the inference that agoraphobia is a fear of being out in public?**
   F Sentence 2
   G Sentence 3
   H Sentence 4
   J Sentence 5

**JUDGE THE EVIDENCE** When you draw conclusions, you have to weigh the evidence. Choose the best answer.

1. **Which statement does NOT support the conclusion that Sarah Brookes' symptoms had been real?**
   A She didn't like being in new situations.
   B She liked feeling out of control.
   C As a child, she didn't relate well to other children.
   D Her fears grew as she got older.

2. **Which statement best supports the conclusion that people can get over phobias?**
   F Van Patten didn't want to be on medication.
   G Van Patten feared his fans.
   H After two years, Van Patten's faith and determination helped him improve.
   J Van Patten started avoiding pressure situations.

**YOUR OWN CONCLUSION** Do you think phobias are real? State your conclusions and support them with examples from both stories.

_____

_____

_____

_____

_____

# Words-per-Minute Table

If you were timed while reading, find your reading time in the column on the left. Find the unit and number of the story across the top of the chart. Follow the time row across to its intersection with the column of the story. This is your reading speed. Go to the next page to plot your progress.

| Unit | 1 | 1 | 2 | 2 | 3 | 3 | 4 | 4 | 5 | 5 | 6 | 6 | 7 | 7 | 8 | 8 | 9 | 9 | 10 | 10 |
|---|---|---|---|---|---|---|---|---|---|---|---|---|---|---|---|---|---|---|---|---|
| **Selection** | 1 | 2 | 1 | 2 | 1 | 2 | 1 | 2 | 1 | 2 | 1 | 2 | 1 | 2 | 1 | 2 | 1 | 2 | 1 | 2 |
| **Word count** | 844 | 841 | 757 | 824 | 775 | 874 | 762 | 944 | 851 | 862 | 794 | 867 | 871 | 783 | 885 | 830 | 772 | 770 | 860 | 797 |
| **Time** | | | | | | | | | | | | | | | | | | | | |
| 1:20 | 633 | 631 | 568 | 618 | 581 | 656 | 572 | 708 | 638 | 647 | 596 | 650 | 653 | 587 | 664 | 623 | 579 | 578 | 645 | 598 |
| 1:40 | 506 | 504 | 454 | 494 | 465 | 524 | 457 | 566 | 510 | 517 | 476 | 520 | 522 | 470 | 531 | 498 | 463 | 462 | 516 | 478 |
| 2:00 | 422 | 421 | 379 | 412 | 388 | 437 | 381 | 472 | 426 | 431 | 397 | 434 | 436 | 392 | 443 | 415 | 386 | 385 | 430 | 399 |
| 2:20 | 362 | 360 | 324 | 353 | 332 | 375 | 327 | 405 | 365 | 369 | 340 | 372 | 373 | 336 | 379 | 356 | 331 | 330 | 369 | 342 |
| 2:40 | 316 | 315 | 284 | 309 | 291 | 328 | 286 | 354 | 319 | 323 | 298 | 325 | 327 | 294 | 332 | 311 | 289 | 289 | 322 | 299 |
| 3:00 | 281 | 280 | 252 | 275 | 258 | 291 | 254 | 315 | 284 | 287 | 265 | 289 | 290 | 261 | 295 | 277 | 257 | 257 | 287 | 266 |
| 3:20 | 253 | 252 | 227 | 247 | 233 | 262 | 229 | 283 | 255 | 259 | 238 | 260 | 261 | 235 | 266 | 249 | 232 | 231 | 258 | 239 |
| 3:40 | 230 | 229 | 206 | 225 | 211 | 238 | 208 | 257 | 232 | 235 | 217 | 236 | 238 | 214 | 241 | 226 | 211 | 210 | 235 | 217 |
| 4:00 | 211 | 210 | 189 | 206 | 194 | 219 | 191 | 236 | 213 | 216 | 199 | 217 | 218 | 196 | 221 | 208 | 193 | 193 | 215 | 199 |
| 4:20 | 195 | 194 | 175 | 190 | 179 | 202 | 176 | 218 | 196 | 199 | 183 | 200 | 201 | 181 | 204 | 192 | 178 | 178 | 198 | 184 |
| 4:40 | 181 | 180 | 162 | 177 | 166 | 187 | 163 | 202 | 182 | 185 | 170 | 186 | 187 | 168 | 190 | 178 | 165 | 165 | 184 | 171 |
| 5:00 | 169 | 168 | 151 | 165 | 155 | 175 | 152 | 189 | 170 | 172 | 159 | 173 | 174 | 157 | 177 | 166 | 154 | 154 | 172 | 159 |
| 5:20 | 158 | 158 | 142 | 155 | 145 | 164 | 143 | 177 | 160 | 162 | 149 | 163 | 163 | 147 | 166 | 156 | 145 | 144 | 161 | 149 |
| 5:40 | 149 | 148 | 134 | 145 | 137 | 154 | 134 | 167 | 150 | 152 | 140 | 153 | 154 | 138 | 156 | 146 | 136 | 136 | 152 | 141 |
| 6:00 | 141 | 140 | 126 | 137 | 129 | 146 | 127 | 157 | 142 | 144 | 132 | 145 | 145 | 131 | 148 | 138 | 129 | 128 | 143 | 133 |
| 6:20 | 133 | 133 | 120 | 130 | 122 | 138 | 120 | 149 | 134 | 136 | 125 | 137 | 138 | 124 | 140 | 131 | 122 | 122 | 136 | 126 |
| 6:40 | 127 | 126 | 114 | 124 | 116 | 131 | 114 | 142 | 128 | 129 | 119 | 130 | 131 | 117 | 133 | 124 | 116 | 115 | 129 | 120 |
| 7:00 | 121 | 120 | 108 | 118 | 111 | 125 | 109 | 135 | 122 | 123 | 113 | 124 | 124 | 112 | 126 | 119 | 110 | 110 | 123 | 114 |
| 7:20 | 115 | 115 | 103 | 112 | 106 | 119 | 104 | 129 | 116 | 118 | 108 | 118 | 119 | 107 | 121 | 113 | 105 | 105 | 117 | 109 |
| 7:40 | 110 | 110 | 99 | 107 | 101 | 114 | 99 | 123 | 111 | 112 | 104 | 113 | 114 | 102 | 115 | 108 | 101 | 100 | 112 | 104 |
| 8:00 | 106 | 105 | 95 | 103 | 97 | 109 | 95 | 118 | 106 | 108 | 99 | 108 | 109 | 98 | 111 | 104 | 97 | 96 | 108 | 100 |
| 8:20 | 101 | 101 | 91 | 99 | 93 | 105 | 91 | 113 | 102 | 103 | 95 | 104 | 105 | 94 | 106 | 100 | 93 | 92 | 103 | 96 |
| 8:40 | 97 | 97 | 87 | 95 | 89 | 101 | 88 | 109 | 98 | 99 | 92 | 100 | 100 | 90 | 102 | 96 | 89 | 89 | 99 | 92 |
| 9:00 | 94 | 93 | 84 | 92 | 86 | 97 | 85 | 105 | 95 | 96 | 88 | 96 | 97 | 87 | 98 | 92 | 86 | 86 | 96 | 89 |
| 9:20 | 90 | 90 | 81 | 88 | 83 | 94 | 82 | 101 | 91 | 92 | 85 | 93 | 93 | 84 | 95 | 89 | 83 | 83 | 92 | 85 |
| 9:40 | 87 | 87 | 78 | 85 | 80 | 90 | 79 | 98 | 88 | 89 | 82 | 90 | 90 | 81 | 92 | 86 | 80 | 80 | 89 | 82 |
| 10:00 | 84 | 84 | 76 | 82 | 78 | 87 | 76 | 94 | 85 | 86 | 79 | 87 | 87 | 78 | 89 | 83 | 77 | 77 | 86 | 80 |
| 10:20 | 82 | 81 | 73 | 80 | 75 | 85 | 74 | 91 | 82 | 83 | 77 | 84 | 84 | 76 | 86 | 80 | 75 | 75 | 83 | 77 |
| 10:40 | 79 | 79 | 71 | 77 | 73 | 82 | 71 | 88 | 80 | 81 | 74 | 81 | 82 | 73 | 83 | 78 | 72 | 72 | 81 | 75 |
| 11:00 | 77 | 76 | 69 | 75 | 70 | 79 | 69 | 86 | 77 | 78 | 72 | 79 | 79 | 71 | 80 | 75 | 70 | 70 | 78 | 72 |
| 11:20 | 74 | 74 | 67 | 73 | 68 | 77 | 67 | 83 | 75 | 76 | 70 | 77 | 77 | 69 | 78 | 73 | 68 | 68 | 76 | 70 |
| 11:40 | 72 | 72 | 65 | 71 | 66 | 75 | 65 | 81 | 73 | 74 | 68 | 74 | 75 | 67 | 76 | 71 | 66 | 66 | 74 | 68 |
| 12:00 | 70 | 70 | 63 | 69 | 65 | 73 | 64 | 79 | 71 | 72 | 66 | 72 | 73 | 65 | 74 | 69 | 64 | 64 | 72 | 66 |
| 12:20 | 68 | 68 | 61 | 67 | 63 | 71 | 62 | 77 | 69 | 70 | 64 | 70 | 71 | 63 | 72 | 67 | 63 | 62 | 70 | 65 |
| 12:40 | 67 | 66 | 60 | 65 | 61 | 69 | 60 | 75 | 67 | 68 | 63 | 68 | 69 | 62 | 70 | 66 | 61 | 61 | 68 | 63 |
| 13:00 | 65 | 65 | 58 | 63 | 60 | 67 | 59 | 73 | 65 | 66 | 61 | 67 | 67 | 60 | 68 | 64 | 59 | 59 | 66 | 61 |
| 13:20 | 63 | 63 | 57 | 62 | 58 | 66 | 57 | 71 | 64 | 65 | 60 | 65 | 65 | 59 | 66 | 62 | 58 | 58 | 65 | 60 |
| 13:40 | 62 | 62 | 55 | 60 | 57 | 64 | 56 | 69 | 62 | 63 | 58 | 63 | 64 | 57 | 65 | 61 | 56 | 56 | 63 | 58 |
| 14:00 | 60 | 60 | 54 | 59 | 55 | 62 | 54 | 67 | 61 | 62 | 57 | 62 | 62 | 56 | 63 | 59 | 55 | 55 | 61 | 57 |
| 14:20 | 59 | 59 | 53 | 57 | 54 | 61 | 53 | 66 | 59 | 60 | 55 | 60 | 61 | 55 | 62 | 58 | 54 | 54 | 60 | 56 |
| 14:40 | 58 | 57 | 52 | 56 | 53 | 60 | 52 | 64 | 58 | 59 | 54 | 59 | 59 | 53 | 60 | 57 | 53 | 52 | 58 | 54 |
| 15:00 | 56 | 56 | 50 | 55 | 52 | 58 | 51 | 63 | 57 | 57 | 53 | 58 | 58 | 52 | 59 | 55 | 51 | 51 | 57 | 53 |

# Plotting Your Progress: Reading Speed

Enter your words-per-minute rate in the box above the appropriate lesson. Then place a small X on the line directly above the number of the lesson, across from the number of words per minute you read. Graph your progress by drawing a line to connect the X's.

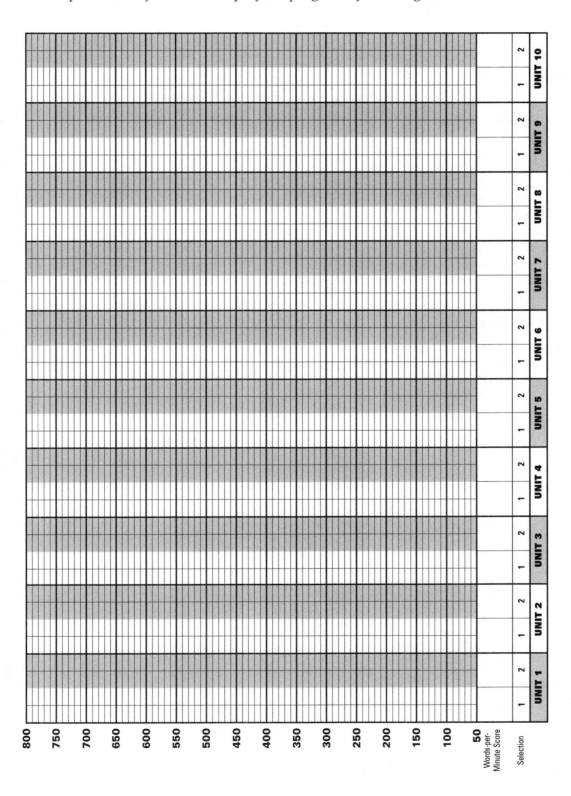

# Photo Credits

Unit 1: p. vi Paul Fosbury/PictureQuest
Unit 1: p. 4 Peter Samuels/Gettyimages
Unit 2: p. 12 Christoph Wilhelm/Gettyimages
Unit 2: p. 16 Gary Morrison/Gettyimages
Unit 3: p. 24 Matthias Clamer/Gettyimages
Unit 3: p. 28 Neville Dawson/PictureQuest
Unit 4: p. 36 Bill Market/PictureQuest
Unit 4: p. 40 Joseph Van Os/Gettyimages
Unit 5: p. 48 Patricia Katchur/Gettyimages
Unit 5: p. 52 Richard Hamilton Smith/Corbis
Unit 6: p. 60 Gettyimages
Unit 6: p. 64 Gettyimages
Unit 7: p. 72 Philip Gould/Corbis
Unit 7: p. 76 Dennis Galante/Gettyimages
Unit 8: p. 84 Roger Ressmeyer/Corbis
Unit 8: p. 88 Andy Roberts/Gettyimages
Unit 9: p. 96 Barry Blackman/Gettyimages
Unit 9: p. 100 Ken Kochey/Gettyimages
Unit 10: p. 108 Robert Daly/Gettyimages
Unit 10: p. 112 PictureQuest